you are is plenty and that what you dream for your family is not only doable, it's the stuff that traditions are made of. You can make beautiful memories, Mom!"

—KENDRA FLETCHER
MOM OF 8 AND AUTHOR, *LOST AND FOUND*

"In an age of Pinterest perfection that makes mothering far too complicated, *Memory-Making Mom* shows how a mom can use her natural rhythms and gifts to create meaningful family traditions without losing her mind. Not only has Jessica provided a wonderfully curated list of new ideas for the big moments of life, such as holidays and birthdays, she's also revealed how the smaller, everyday milestones can be celebrated and marked in the minds of those a mother loves most."

—JAMIE ERICKSON
THE UNLIKELY HOMESCHOOL CREATOR AND
AUTHOR, *HOMESCHOOL BRAVELY*

"This book is a must-read for every mom who wants to make special memories with her kids but feels overwhelmed by her Pinterest boards and social media feeds. I am that mom, but I now feel equipped to make small changes that will have a big impact. Jessica inspires us to give thought, time, and effort to enriching our family's memories with traditions, and then she provides page after page of practical suggestions to help us get started. With Jessica's help we all can be memory-making moms!"

—MARISSA HENLEY
AUTHOR, *LOVING YOUR FRIEND THROUGH CANCER*

Praise for *Memory-Making Mom*

"As I ponder the life-giving memories that weave throughout my own family's tapestry, it's almost always the simple and meaningful traditions our five children treasure most. Jessica's warm storytelling, inspiration, and intentional ideas woven throughout *Memory-Making Mom* give all of us simple steps to create the home for which we've always longed. This book is a gift to all families."

—JEN SCHMIDT
AUTHOR, *JUST OPEN THE DOOR*, THE BECOMING CONFERENCE
HOST, AND BALANCING BEAUTY AND BEDLAM BLOGGER

"On behalf of moms everywhere I want to thank Jessica Smartt for writing *Memory-Making Mom*. Nothing about this book feels burdensome or overwhelming, rather doable and exciting!

"We moms want to make meaningful memories with our kids, but sometimes the thought of planning traditions feels more like a burden than a blessing. Cue *Memory-Making Mom*! This is the most readable and enjoyable book on the market for overwhelmed moms who love the snot out of their kids. Reading it, one short chapter at a time, feels like rest rather than another chore. And putting it into practice will breathe life into your busy life. Guaranteed."

—WENDY SPEAKE
COAUTHOR, *TRIGGERS*

"*Memory-Making Mom* is a gift to this generation of mothers. With so many things demanding our energy, we desperately need the reminder to zero in on what's important. Jessica speaks the perfect mix of grace ("you can't do it all") and challenge ("you *can* do something"), which is exactly what I needed. This book has changed how we do things around our house, and I'm excited for the many other mothers and homes it will benefit."

—KATIE BENNETT
EMBRACINGASIMPLERLIFE.COM CREATOR AND
AUTHOR, *HEAVENLY MINDED MOM*

"*Memory-Making Mom* hooked me as soon as I read Jessica's guilt-free disclaimer on page one. As a perfectionist who tends to turn everything into a must-do, I needed that permission slip to breathe easy. I also needed her reminder to revel in ordinary adventures and then her gentle push to get out the door and try something new—something that could end up being one of my children's, and my own, favorite memory decades from now."

—JAMIE C. MARTIN

SIMPLEHOMESCHOOL.NET EDITOR AND

AUTHOR, *GIVE YOUR CHILD THE WORLD*

"In the busyness of motherhood it can often feel as if the meaningful moments have been squeezed right out of everyday life. But it is never too late to refocus and make a change. Filled with wisdom and an overflow of practical ideas, *Memory-Making Mom* is that personal guide we all need on this journey toward a more intentional family life."

—RUTH SCHWENK

THEBETTERMOM.COM FOUNDER AND AUTHOR, *PRESSING PAUSE, THE BETTER MOM, AND FOR BETTER OR FOR KIDS*

"While reading *Memory-Making Mom*, Jessica Smartt reignited my passion to create happy memories with my children. I've been parenting for twenty-five years and have kept up a high level of intention throughout. But many of the ideas she includes were new to me and sparked fresh energy for intentional memory-making with my children. I especially loved the call to make even work or rest days memorable. I'll be reading this book on repeat until my kids are grown."

—JENNIFER PEPITO

THE PEACEFUL PRESS FOUNDER

"For every twinge of mom guilt that you just aren't doing enough, for every time you've thought of going big but just couldn't pull it together, for every holiday that left you flattened instead of more in love with your family, Jessica has written these words of grace and encouragement just for you. *Memory-Making Mom* will lovingly remind you that who

MEMORY-MAKING MOM

BUILDING TRADITIONS THAT
BREATHE LIFE INTO YOUR HOME

JESSICA SMARTT

W PUBLISHING GROUP

AN IMPRINT OF THOMAS NELSON

Published in Nashville, Tennessee, by W Publishing Group, an imprint of Thomas Nelson.

Published in association with William K. Jensen Literary Agency, 119 Bampton Court, Eugene, Oregon 97404.

Thomas Nelson titles may be purchased in bulk for educational, business, fund-raising, or sales promotional use. For information, please e-mail SpecialMarkets@ThomasNelson.com.

Unless otherwise noted, Scripture quotations are taken from the Holy Bible, New International Version®, NIV®. © 1973, 1978, 1984, 2011 by Biblica, Inc.® Used by permission of Zondervan. All rights reserved worldwide.

Scripture quotations marked ESV are from the ESV® Bible (The Holy Bible, English Standard Version®). © 2001 by Crossway, a publishing ministry of Good News Publishers. Used by permission. All rights reserved.

Scripture quotations marked NKJV are from the New King James Version®. © 1982 by Thomas Nelson. Used by permission. All rights reserved.

Any Internet addresses, phone numbers, or company or product information printed in this book are offered as a resource and are not intended in any way to be or to imply an endorsement by Thomas Nelson, nor does Thomas Nelson vouch for the existence, content, or services of these sites, phone numbers, companies, or products beyond the life of this book.

ISBN 978-0-7852-2118-0 (eBook)

Library of Congress Cataloging-in-Publication Data

Names: Smartt, Jessica, author.
Title: Memory-making mom : building traditions that breathe life into your home / Jessica Smartt, Jessica Smartt.
Description: Nashville : Thomas Nelson, 2019.
Identifiers: LCCN 2018041908| ISBN 9780785221227 (paperback) | ISBN 9780785221180 (E-book)
Subjects: LCSH: Families. | Parenting. | Motherhood.
Classification: LCC HQ519 .S626 2019 | DDC 306.85--dc23 LC record available at https://lccn.loc.gov/2018041908

Printed in the United States of America

23 24 25 26 27 LBC 7 6 5 4 3

To Todd: I'd marry you again in a heartbeat.
And to Sam, Ty, and Ellie, my three greatest gifts.

CONTENTS

CONTENTS

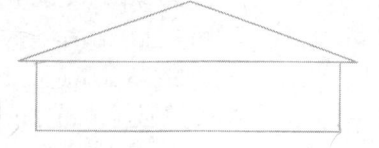

BEFORE YOU READ
THIS BOOK

Dear new friend,

Recently I gave a little talk on the topic of traditions. Afterward a mama approached me, choking back tears. She'd had a rough childhood, and the idea of building beautiful traditions with her young family seemed impossible. By the time I finished encouraging her, *another* overwhelmed mom cornered me. She said, "My kids are one and three, and our life is a zoo. How in the *world* can I do all of this stuff?"

I tried to encourage these mamas, but I was shaken. I don't want a book that paints this unattainable picture of supermoms and Miss Perfects. I want *the everyday mom*—you there, you with the oatmeal-crusted bowls in the sink, and the snotty-nosed toddler, and the husband working late, you from a broken home and a lonely neighborhood—*you, the real moms*, I want you to love this book.

So before you read, hear me: *This is a book of suggestions, not a must-do manual.* You can't do them all, nor should you. Every family is different; no family's traditions are the same. I'm going to throw out a lot of ideas in the pages to come. No one could ever do all of them! (And I assured that young mama that I was certainly doing very few of them when I had two toddlers at home.) When you are tempted to despair—"I could never do all this! My home will never look like this!"—then promise me you'll try something. Just one thing. Try saying, "We can't do it all, but we can make our own beautiful memories." Say it aloud, just for practice: "We can't do it all, but we can make our own beautiful memories."

Sweet memory-making mom, that is my hope for you. I hope this book reminds you just how beautiful it can be when families make memories together. I hope that some of these treasured memories become *traditions*, repeated and longed for year after year. And on the days when you feel like you've got the gumption to make a new memory, to start a new tradition, may this book be the first place you look.

Memory-making right alongside you,
Jessica

P.S.: For quick reference, you can find most of the specific traditions I mention throughout the book, plus many more, in the 200+ Great Memory-Making Ideas appendix. And be sure to check out my best memory-making resources at **www.smarttereachday.com/ memorymakingmomresources**.

CHAPTER 1

THE WORST DAY, THE BEST GIFT

You are what you remember.

—SALLY CLARKSON[1]

THREE YEARS AGO, ON A BEAUTIFUL SUNDAY IN JUNE, we nearly lost our son. For all of the scheming, controlling, and protecting I have done for his entire life, this time—the worst time—it was my fault. Me, the mom. My fault he had an allergic reaction requiring four EpiPen injections. My fault we rode in the ambulance. My fault we spent two days in the ICU. I was the one who made his oatmeal, made the other oatmeal, confused them, didn't watch.

There was a lot of guilt.

There was a lot of fear. So, so much fear. A large load of it, as you'd imagine, over things like, *How do we actually go on? How do we live knowing one single bite of the wrong food could do this?*

There was something else, though.

Late that evening, I sat in the hospital recliner, feet tucked under me, listening to the beeps and hums of medical equipment. I watched his little sleeping chest rise and fall rhythmically. (Thank You, Jesus.) In the first dark calm of the whole horrible day, a different kind of fear swept over me. It wasn't fear of losing him. *It was fear of parenting with deep regret.* I saw the last six years of his little life playing like a movie in my head. Where was I in that movie? I was rushing. I didn't make eye contact; I was busy. I was on my phone a lot. The days were mostly slurred together in one long monotonous blur.

I sat in that awful hospital room and wept. Wept for the stupid allergies, yes, but wept for my missed chances. And, I realized through sobs, I was terrified. I was terrified, of course, of losing our son. *Lord, please help us; he is in Your hands.* But I was also terrified of him living, and me texting, hurrying, cleaning, and rushing through his childhood. We did not lose our son that day. But if we had? And those six years that felt like a snap of the fingers—what if *that* was our chance at parenting? The rush of regret was nearly palpable.

> I want my children to know they are loved, to know what they believe, and to have the tools they need to succeed.

I feared this song would play on repeat through all three of our children's lives. I feared we would feel that same sense of crushing incompleteness eighteen years later, closing the door to some safety award-winning sedan in which we'd packed their stuff, kissing them through the window, and watching them drive off to a dorm room or apartment somewhere. The car would dim out of view, and we'd feel terrible remorse at the opportunities we had missed to make memories that matter.

I want to parent well.

I want to send my children off with memories for roots, love for wings. I want my children to know they are loved, to know what they believe, and to have the tools they need to succeed. I don't want any regrets.

In a strange way, this allergic reaction was a gift. A wake-up call, as those ambulance-ride kind of days tend to

> Gradually, the answer came to me: what our family needed was traditions.

be. I knew we needed a change. But how? Gradually, the answer came to me: what our family needed was traditions.

TRADITIONS: THE ANSWER WE DIDN'T KNOW WE NEEDED

I know it seems a curious answer at first. How could chipped ceramic plates with painted-on rabbits, that "same old" devotional book fished from under the bed each night, pizza on paper plates every Friday . . . how could these trifles satisfy the deep longings we have for our children? These things are little, insignificant nothings. Yet grouped together, repeated over and over, expected and longed for week after week, Christmas after Christmas—these rituals tell a story, make a childhood, bind a family, build a faith.

I knew this was true when I watched my sister and her family. They seemed to celebrate everything with whimsy and inexplicable energy. Friday night? Pizza time! Saint Patrick's Day? Beer bread and shepherd's pie! Snow day? The legendary snowman pancakes of course! And on and on. It was insanely annoying to watch, like a real-live Pinterest explosion three houses down from my own.

I couldn't articulate it, but I wanted my life—our family—to be more like that. While our months seemed to drone on, theirs were punctuated with special, predictable traditions. Fun, basically. They were having more fun.

It took some time, but slowly it dawned on me there was no

reason we couldn't also become a traditions family. Sure, I was a little late to the ball game, but who cares? Couldn't we still give it a shot? As these things tend to go, the kids were not in the slightest reticent to try some of my new changes. They received every new celebration and family ritual with childhood elation.

As our home has become filled with more "specials" and more exclamations of "today's the day!" I have seen with my own eyes the gifts that come from being a tradition-family.

WHAT IS A TRADITION?

There are plenty of long, fancy definitions for *tradition*, but I think of it simply: traditions are a planned determination to remember, celebrate, and value what is important.

The fun things. The special things. The meaning things. The things with truth and goodness and warmth. Traditions vary from person to person, family to family, culture to culture. And that's the beauty; we decide what is meaningful, and we celebrate it.

As I think to my own childhood, few traditions were more wonderful than our yearly beach vacation to Daytona Beach, Florida. I can tell you exactly when it started. One day we kids were eating tuna-fish sandwiches at the beat-up oak kitchen table when Mom asked, "Guys, how would you like to go to Daytona Beach with your cousins this summer?"

> Traditions are a planned determination to remember, celebrate, and value what is important.

Waves of prepubescent joy shot through my body. Our cousins and dearest friends in the whole world? Could anything be more exciting? It absolutely could not. We had been to Daytona Beach for the past two summers, but to have our dearest cousin-friends digging holes in the sand with us, drinking nonalcoholic strawberry daiquiris on vinyl lounge chairs, and correcting one-piece bathing suit wedgies from too much boogie boarding—guys, this was all almost too exciting to imagine. This was the pinnacle of life, right here. I had reached euphoria at ten years old.

Our two families lived four states away, so we had to share our joy long distance. We wrote giddy letters back and forth for months (the real kind, with stamps and misspellings and purple Lisa Frank stickers). As the week neared, we'd go shopping for a brand-new outfit, maybe two if we were lucky. One year I got purple and green shorts with daisy appliques. I think I refolded them a dozen times in my suitcase to make sure the daisies didn't crumple the wrong way, you know, in transit. Years later when I gushed to my husband, Todd, about Daytona Beach, he said it sounded like I was confused and was instead describing Bermuda.

Daytona was the highlight of every year, the best part of every summer. One year Uncle Joe burned blisters on his feet from walking three miles in the sand to eat oysters. One year there were wildfires in Florida, and we couldn't get a tan (cue teenage heartbreak) because the cloud of ashes was so thick it'd drop pieces of soot on our towels. That year was a bust. But we went back every summer for ten years. It was tradition.

I doubt my parents ever sat down with bullet-point lists and parental intention as they resolved, "We need a tradition. Let's make it Daytona Beach, every last week in June." As with many traditions, it grew in importance. Maybe you remember a few of your own from your childhood. More likely than not, you have some right now with your own family—maybe some you haven't even realized are traditions.

I don't know what prompted you to pick up this book. Maybe you've been longing for more richness and more celebrating in your home. Maybe your family has had its own wake-up-call experience, like our son's allergic reaction, and you've resolved to be more intentional about the things that matter. Whatever your story, I believe that the message of this book can change the course of your family. I believe that five, ten, or twenty years later, the traditions you start now can be some of your family's most treasured memories. I'm here to hold your hand as we dream about what this could look like for your family.

CHAPTER 2

WHY I IRON THE NAPKINS

All the Hard Work Is Worth It

How precious a thing is the human family.
Is it not worth some sacrifice in time,
energy, safety, discomfort, and work?

—EDITH SCHAEFFER[1]

IF YOU'RE LIKE ME, TRADITIONS SOUND DREAMY IN theory, but the reality of implementing them makes you want to curl up for a nap. At some point, you're going to look at a wrinkly tablecloth jammed in a linen closet, cracker crumbs all over the floor, the un-browned beef that was supposed to be a pot roast dinner, and you will think something along the lines of, *Never mind that stupid traditions book. I am exhausted. Traditions are dumb.* (Not that I have ever thought this, but so I've heard.)

At that point you have a choice to make. You can call it quits and feed everyone frozen waffles in front of the TV, or you can pull together the few remaining shreds of energy you have and make some tradition magic. I'm here to make the case against the waffles.

Now, that's not to say a mama doesn't need a break every so often (more on that later). And no disrespect to frozen waffles, which have an accumulated specialness of their own. But there is a point we cannot avoid: keeping good rituals alive takes work. We need a *why* to keep us motivated. Let's talk about the why.

TRADITIONS OFFER SECURITY

When we facilitate traditions, we create stability and security for children as well as adults. In *Treasuring God in Our Traditions*, Noël Piper relays the story of a friend who had a difficult and un-satisfying childhood, but every year, without fail, there were staple holiday traditions: the red Jell-O mold for Christmas, the paltry potato salad for Easter. These insignificant rituals were predictable and comforting even though the spiritual aspects of her family life were lacking.[2]

There is something innate in us humans that craves routine. We are made in the image of the One who created the hours and rhythmic seasons and makes the sun rise every blessed day. We find comfort in the repetition and the counted-on. Especially our little ones. If you have any sort of regular family ritual, you probably already know exactly what I mean. Do your little ones erupt with joy when they realize, *Today! Today is the day!*

My kids do that with Saturday morning pancakes. This was one of our first traditions, which I was hesitant to start because I thought, *Saturdays are so busy. We'll never be able to keep up with it.* Oh, but we do! They'll never let me forget that Saturday mornings exist only for blueberry pancakes, crispy bacon, scrambled eggs, and orange slices. One week, as a tradition novice, I made the mistake of trying to serve oatmeal. There was a near mutiny. They literally squeal in ecstasy when they see the griddle on the counter. Is it that our breakfast life is that pathetic the other six days? Are my pancakes the fluffiest and most decadent pastries known to man? You would think so, but I assure you that is not the case. *It is not the pancakes. It's the ritual.*

When I was very young, my dad traveled a lot. I hated that he left, but I knew that he would bring back a treat for us when he traveled. I missed him terribly; I would sneak into my parents' bedroom late at night and smell his pillow for the lingering cologne. But when we finally heard the door crack open and bags drop to the foyer floor, we would scurry in and scream, "What did you bring us?!" Because there was always something. I hardly remember the gifts, weirdly. A butterscotch lollipop, maybe? A Matchbox car? It mattered little. We simply knew he would come home, and there'd be a treat waiting. There is just nothing like a predictable ritual.

TRADITIONS PROVIDE COMFORTING MEMORIES

Traditions create positive memories we can draw on during times of sadness, temptation, or loneliness. They are a way of intentionally packing a box of memories for our kids to take with them when they leave home. We must be intentional to fill their boxes with verses memorized, foods relished, adventures made, beauty seen.

My box of memories helped me when I was a lonely, awkward college freshman living five hundred miles from home. No lie. I endured those first few dreadful weeks solely by remembering Thanksgiving. Sure, I was showering in my flip-flops (weird), sleeping across the room from a total stranger, and eating under-salted beef goulash for dinner. But no worries; in a few short months, I'd pull up a chair between my cousins and sisters at the massive family table, and we'd eat mashed potato stuffing and apple crumb pie until we had to unbutton our jeans. College? I could make it. Baby steps.

You never know what traditions your children will treasure the rest of their lives. One child may grow up regaling his kids about the special red plate that he always got on his birthday. Another might insist on Monday spaghetti night for the rest of history. Another might remember the special back rubs when she was sick, the warm apple cider by the fire . . . who knows what memory-seeds will grow into big oak trees of joy and comfort in their souls?

TRADITIONS MAKE LIFE SPARKLE

Traditions insert spark and fun into the mundane monotony of life. Need proof? Watch a child's face when you drag a seven-foot-tall pine tree over the oriental rug and plop it next to the coffee table. Pure magic! The week before Christmas we dress the kids in their warmest pajamas, sprint to the van, layer fuzzy blankets and stuffed animals on top of them in their car seats, and drive around to look at Christmas lights. The first year I tried to serve hot chocolate and candy canes on the ride, but after cleaning gelat-inized chocolate goo out of car seat crevices and candy canes out of ponytails, I opted to put that aspect of the tradition on temporary hold. Besides, twenty-feet-tall inflatable reindeer whose heads turn back and forth are special enough when you're three years old. No need for refreshments, really. It's a glorified car ride, but to them it's magical. Traditions impart a spark of fun, brightness, and joy to break the monotony of life.

TRADITIONS REMIND US WHAT MATTERS

I love hymns, and a few years ago I attempted to institute "family hymn sing" in the mornings. I wanted those rich, old words as daily reminders of our faith. Of course, family hymn sing sounds quite romantic, doesn't it? But for the first three months, I was literally singing to myself. It was just me and the kids because my husband had already left for work. They would mumble, collapse on the table like their upper bodies had turned to mush, roll their eyes, chatter through it.

After eight faithful weeks I had one convert: the two-year-old, who surprisingly learned a fair portion of the first stanza of "Joyful, Joyful We Adore Thee." Eventually she rubbed off on her two older brothers, one of whom, after four solid months of my solos, wondered aloud one morning, "Hey, aren't we going to sing today?" All of which is a strong testament to the need for steady perseverance in the face of children who appear to be sleeping or suffering through your important things. We all enjoy it now, and they're learning the words, and I even hear them humming hymns as they're swinging on the swing set or playing with LEGOs. It took work, but I knew hymns and their rich wording were important, so I kept at it. And every time we sing, we have the reminder of God's love. *Traditions make us remember.*

TRADITIONS MAKE OUR VALUES REAL

Traditions make us *implement* what is important. What I mean here is that it's one thing to say you value something, but to do it regularly takes a different sort of gumption. Maybe I am just extra lazy, but I'm afraid that if church were not a thing, for example, and I had to randomly muster up the energy on any given day to bathe, dress, corral my children and their seventeen various required bags, drive across town, and keep them quiet and still for ninety minutes that can feel like seven hours *whenever we felt like it*, we would rarely go. But church *is* a thing. It's a Sunday thing, and we do it every single week. The tradition makes the important happen.

When we complained about rules as kids, my mom would explain that rules were like the fence, and we had the whole big, safe yard to play in. The fence made life better.

I think it's kind of like that with traditions. They show you the way, and then the hard work is done. Okay, I'm lying . . . we're parents; it's all hard work. But you know what is different? Instead of harboring a vague, guilty, we-really-should-do-that-sometime feeling, you will have a satisfying plan.

I know all this "you'll feel better" talk may sound fuzzy, but I can promise you it is really, deeply true. When it dawned on me that my family was lacking meaningful traditions and I began to implement some, I honestly felt better laying my head on my pillow at night. Much of the guilt and angst I felt under the surface disappeared as I had a plan for the important things in life. When I feel that mom guilt and angst creeping back in, my traditions are what ground me. Motherhood angst usually means I've lost my way somehow—forgotten or stopped doing some of the rituals that mean the most to our family. And so we bring them back.

TRADITIONS CONNECT US TO OTHERS

Traditions are a bonding agent that keep families and generations connected. They connect us to the past, present, and future generations and cultures. I know these last two sentences aren't the sexiest things you've read all day. We moderns love to be independent and stand-alone sufficient. I had a college professor who nailed it: our culture is rampant with "generational discrimination."[3] If it's old, we don't want it. What a shame! I do love the strides of my century (with a head nod to my best friend, the washing machine). But there are many treasures of the past I long to pass on to my children, and traditions are the way to do it.

When we recite the Lord's Prayer, we're connecting with our brothers in Indonesia, and our brothers in the seventh century, and the poor in Ethiopia, and the wealthy in New York . . . we are all connected, through our tradition. When we light candles on Christmas Eve or wave flags and light fireworks, we are all connected. Traditions are the great connector. They draw us out of the me-centered worlds we tend to live in and remind us of something greater than our own little selves, greater than our day-to-day lives and greater than any one single person. Traditions broaden our perspectives.

TRADITIONS SHOWER LOVE

Finally, good traditions make the members of your family feel that they are important and loved. This was something I really did not understand until I started exerting the effort to implement rituals in our home.

The other day, for example, I was cutting clippings from our rosebush for our weekly family dinner tradition. My six-year-old (a boy, mind you) came running over. "What are those for?"

"They're for us," I responded. "To go on the table for family dinner."

His eyes widened, and he ran to his brother. "Mom's putting those flowers on the table for us!"

When my kids see the crisp-ironed tablecloth, the flower-adorned table, the crystal candlesticks, and the real glass mugs filled with their sparkly juice, you can read it in their eyes: *We matter. Our family matters.*

TRADITIONS ARE WORTH IT

Sometimes life has me overwhelmed. Occasionally I'm tempted to throw in the towel on traditions and skip Christmas for a year or something like that. But that's when I try to remember the champions, the pioneers paving the memory-making path before me.

> You can read it in their eyes: *We matter. Our family matters.*

A few years ago my sister Jenny had the kind of week that would have made me disintegrate into a puddle of self-pity. Her entire family was infected with the stomach bug from you-know-where. Her husband barely recovered before he left the country for a week. It was the Christmas season, so she had just had out-of-town guests, and more were coming soon. (Brave guests.) I saw her once, from a distance, and don't tell her, but she looked like she had been run over by a garbage truck, twice. *Exhausted* doesn't even begin to describe it. And who could blame her? I would have crumpled. Yet—she sent me a picture—that very day (the one after the stomach bug) she and her four little kids had cut out snowman accessories and decorated their front door like a happy snowman—a cheery, wintry ray of sunshine.

I stared at this picture of Mr. Front Door Snowman for, like, five minutes. What kind of supernatural being could manage to cut construction-paper carrot noses mere hours after the stomach bug? It was baffling, but at the same time I understood. This little winter craft was their own determination to celebrate Christmas, *even if.* To say, in their own way, that Christmas was worth fighting for. It was crystal clear to Jenny: This is worth it. The kids are worth it. The season is worth it.

I know this can feel overwhelming, and at times it's a heavy load to carry. It takes so much work to be a memory-making mom! But we do not set down the load because the journey is tiring. When something is worth it, we work for it.

We can celebrate with whimsy. We can make memories. We can create treasured traditions our children will lie in bed and anticipate, tell their children about, long for during college, and cling to in times of sadness. When a special moment arrives, snatch the opportunity and create a memory that is important and lasting.

There is something about saying, "We always do this," which helps keep the years together. Time is such an elusive thing that if we keep on meaning to do something interesting but never do it, year would follow year with no special thoughtfulness being expressed in making gifts, surprises, charming table settings, and familiar food.[4]

CHAPTER 3

SPONTANEITY

Let's Go on an Adventure

*Twenty years from now you will be more
disappointed by the things that you didn't
do than by the ones you did do.*

—H. JACKSON BROWN JR.[1]

FIVE YEARS AGO I WROTE A BLOG POST CALLED "GIVE Them the Simple Life." It was a plea to parents not to go overboard, to realize that their kids don't really need all the excursions and experiences that we feel we have to give them. I boasted in my post, "Stop running around like a crazy person to give them everything! The simple life is all they need!" That sort of thing.

Between you and me, we were darn near poor when I wrote this post, and I was jealous—plain and simple. All my friends' kids, it seemed, were riding elephants at the circus or snorkeling in the Bahamas. Meanwhile, mine were in the backyard painting the porch with water and crusty old paintbrushes.

I think I had a point. After all, I do remember my own porch-painting days rather fondly. I have relished many a snack box of store-brand raisins on a falling-apart backyard hammock. I am who I am, really, because of snuggling on beat-up sofas, eating canned chicken soup with crackers, coloring with broken Crayola crayons, and other such small pleasures. Simple is good.

Here is the thing, though, that started nagging at me disconcertedly after I hit Publish. While I love a good ordinary day, the fact cannot be ignored that I also treasure quite a few special childhood memories. The totally unusual, random, spontaneous, extravagant, crazy, once-in-a-lifetime experiences. Getting picked up by my grandparents in their huge motorhome to go camping. The date with my parents at a white-napkin, candlelit restaurant for my thirteenth birthday. Biking with my cousins on "the real roads" (read: *Dangerous! So dangerous!*) to eat chicken fingers at Dixie Joe's restaurant. The magical day it snowed twelve inches and my dad trudged with us through snowy fields to eat snacks at a gas station.

These wild, extra-ordinary adventures are so powerful in my memory and have made such a dent in my person that I couldn't ignore their influence. So I started to admit that maybe we need both: the comforting monotony of the everyday as well as spontaneous special days.

The simple times build character. The special times give memories. Kids need both.

THE GIFT OF BECOMING
ADVENTURE-READY

As memory-making mothers, there's no way around it. We must be celebration seekers and adventure experts because traditions don't just announce themselves. They generally become something after the memory is formed. You have to keep your adventure-eyes peeled, so to speak.

I'm not naturally good at this, but I've had my moments. One Sunday afternoon both my husband and I had a bizarre and supernatural gifting of energy. Normally, as parents of young children, Sunday afternoons find us in some version of parental coma and recovery from the week. But this day, both of us seemed oddly alert as we finished lunch. I said to Todd, "We should go climb a mountain."

He looked at me blankly. We did, after all, have a toddler and loads of laundry spewing between us on the couch.

"No, really," I countered. "Are we going to remember today if we sit here in our house? We'll remember it if we go climb a mountain."

In near-miraculous magical performance that I have never rivaled, I whipped up homemade fried chicken and biscuits, cut some watermelon, packed a cooler, and we drove to the nearest mountain.

Since then, it's become a late-summer tradition for our family to climb a mountain. I will go ahead and confess to you that sometimes it's more "take a long walk" than "climb a mountain." That Sunday afternoon, I couldn't have foreseen that we'd want to make it a tradition. It was just a fun idea, but it became a thing.

> The more spontaneous you are in capturing an adventure-moment, the more likely you will be to unearth precious traditions for your family.

I see that pattern often in our most beloved rituals. The more spontaneous you are in capturing an adventure-moment, the more likely you will be to unearth precious traditions for your family. First the crazy thing, then the tradition. Be willing to give those harebrained ideas a go. There's no way to know where a wonderful tradition may be lurking behind some seemingly ridiculous idea.

Like neighborhood church. One winter, we had a blizzard like we've never seen before in our southern state. Guys, this was epic. Any snow is a big deal in the South. With the lightest dusting of snow, stores sell out of bottled water and deprived neighborhood kids go sledding on what is essentially frost. So when I say it was twelve-inches-of-snow epic, it was twelve-inches-of-snow epic. *Elated* doesn't even begin to cover our thrill.

I was standing in nearly new snow boots in the middle of the snow-packed driveway when it hit me: *Churches are canceled. We should do neighborhood church!* In less than twelve hours, we had bulletins, busy bags for the kids, three dozen muffins, and Dunkin' Donuts coffee. We had a preacher, a banjo player, two guitarists, and a living room full of flushed and noisy toddlers. It was the best.

Incidentally, it's snowed on a Sunday every year since then. I don't know how to break it to my children that this is actually not a normal climate occurrence for our region of the country, but we will ride it out while it lasts. And even if it doesn't snow? We have all resolved that neighborhood church is now a thing. It's tradition.

A bunch of overheated kids and a makeshift band in your living room may sound rather nightmarish to you. The point isn't this particular event, but that moment on the driveway in my snow boots. If I hadn't paid attention to the crazy idea, our whole neighborhood would miss out on a fabulous tradition. See, the very best ideas have a way of hiding in unlikely moments. *Unlikely* is a nice way of saying you may not want to do the thing at all. Yes, often a really good idea, a treasured memory, or a powerful ritual will nudge its way into your subconscious on the days when you've, say . . . machine-washed a disposable diaper, when all five of you have just barely recovered from a horrendous outbreak of strep throat, or when you are so tuckered out, you could nap on the floor of your local Walmart. (*Been there, done that.*) But this is my vote to pay attention to those small, crazy ideas.

THE GIFT OF DOING THE SURPRISING

Here's another thought: If you want to make a real treasured adventure, think of what your default personality is, and then do the opposite.[2] It is guaranteed to be an experience your kids will remember. When we were young, my mom occasionally would hit the brakes on our minivan, pull over to the side of some cow pasture, and holler "Moo!" as fiercely as she could. My demure, quiet mom, mooing at the cattle? We would die laughing!

If you're a reserved homebody—you can probably see where this is going, and you may not like it—pack the kids up in the car and go somewhere totally out of your comfort zone. You know the places . . . the roller rink, one of those bouncy trampoline parks, a water amusement park . . . Is your heart rate sufficiently elevated yet?

If you're a fiery tornado of a mom-on-a-mission, you're not off the hook. Maybe cuddling and reading stories feels difficult for you. Designate a cozy tea time with as many books as they want to read. If you're a mom who hates getting dirty, stomp in the mud with them. If you're not normally a get-dressed-up type of gal but your little sweetheart is, get your nails done together. Maybe these aren't the most suitable examples for you, but you can brainstorm what this might look like for your family. The first step is to think, *What do my kids love to do that I never do with them?* And there, friends, is a sweet spot for memory-making.

Since we were toddlers, my cousin Sheila was always the one *pooh-poohing* my tea party ideas in lieu of some dangerously concocted mission. We were chatting about this adventure concept recently, and Sheila reminded me, "Adventure isn't always safe."[3] Sometimes just past the comfort zone are the precious memories.

> Sometimes just past the comfort zone are the precious memories.

You know those unsafe things we moms tend to frown upon? Hiking up the extra-tall mountain, sledding down the steeper hill, racing your kids on a bike . . . Maybe every so often, do some of those.

THE GIFT OF CHOOSING SPONTANEOUS ADVENTURES

Be an adventure detective. Maybe my ideas of trampoline parks and racing down hills on bikes sound horrible to you. That's okay: make your own adventure. You have the power.

I know well the very strong excuses—no, *excuses* is too weak—the very strong *forces* that work against a mother or father with the most sincere and heartfelt desires for a positive family culture. We all long for it. The memories, the rituals, the cozy and inviting family life. Yet there are always the pressing-in things that make it so difficult.

I recall my mother saying, "The hardest thing about motherhood was the lack of sleep." Before kids, I thought, *How weird! Why in the world would she be so tired? And what does that have to do with anything?* Mom, I am sorry, and I get it.

So many days in my deepest longings I want to pile us in the car and hike a mountain. But in my actual real life I cannot hold my eyes open, so we stay home and fold laundry or something lame like that. There is also the money issue. There have been days when even spontaneous takeout from Chick-fil-A or tickets to the zoo would come at a steep cost to our monthly budget. And believe me when I say I understand the feeling that life is so jam-packed, you simply do not have time for one more adventure.

ADVENTURES ARE WORTH THE COST

The truth is a very real battle is going on in our homes and minivans. Mothers and fathers all over are asking, "Should we _____ today?" (Fill in the blank with some fun idea that you don't feel like doing.) "Is it worth it?"

I am saying yes, one thousand times. The memories are worth it.

One beautiful young lady whom I taught in middle school passed away in a car accident shortly after graduating high school. I saw her dear parents at a wedding about a year later. I was afraid to make them cry, but I wanted to tell them, "I loved that you took so many adventures as a family."

It was true. They took their girls on the most fantastic trips to Spain, New Zealand, Alaska. Nearly every school break had them journeying to some fascinating place. This father looked me straight in the eye, his smile deep with pain. "I always told my wife, 'We only have them for eighteen years.' I didn't realize how true that would be."

When I put a number to it, it lights a fire under me. *Seven summers left with my oldest.* Seven! I promise you, three weeks ago he was teething. My most popular blog post is titled "I Asked Twenty Moms with Grown Kids What They Regret Most; Here Are Their Answers." One woman I surveyed responded, "I always wished we'd gone on more adventures together. But truthfully, I was so tired and overwhelmed!"

I so relate to her—the fatigue and feeling overwhelmed, yet the back-of-the-mind nagging to create memories. There are many days I am just plumb tuckered out with motherhood, so we stay bored and cranky in the same old domestic life. That's part of it. But I think it's surprising how you can—if you try—dig down deep in the well and muster the strength to go adventuring.

Edith Schaeffer reminds us:

> Remember *that you are often choosing a memory.* Many times you are not choosing what to do with two or three hours for the immediate result, but you are choosing a memory (or choosing *not* to have that memory) for a lifetime. . . . The bubble of excitement, the thrill that comes in being loved and considered important, the reality of discovering that our mother and father really like to be together with us . . . will make it a stronger, longer-lasting, and more vivid memory than even the planned days could ever be.[4]

I read this, and I want to shout from the roof, jump out of the pages, and give a warm hug and a steaming cup of coffee to the moms and dads who have pushed past their own schedules and fatigue to make a family memory. You are fighting the good fight, you memory-making mom!

THE GIFT OF REWRITING THE STORY

When we make a memory, something powerful is happening. We are rewriting the story of our families, our own lives. Anyone, anywhere, anytime has this capacity.

I think of my friend Bill, who had a less-than-perfect childhood. He laughs and says his only dinner traditions were hot dogs and bowls of cold cereal. "I raised myself," he says with enough maturity and distance between him and the cold cereal dinners to say it matter-of-factly and even with a little laugh. His is a beautiful redemption story. Today Bill's home is the embodiment of warmth, beloved family, exquisite meals, and savored traditions. Elaborate homemade sugar cookies every Christmas, turkey dinners with Thanksgiving fixings every March (*just because*), classical music and wine on the patio on summer evenings. How did Bill make this change? He decided he could write his own story.

Maybe you're a few years into your own parenting gig and don't have one worthwhile ritual to your name. *You can rewrite the story.*

Maybe you're not creative, not wealthy, parenting solo, or plumb out of energy. *You can rewrite the story.*

Maybe it's been a hard Monday, a hard March, a hard *motherhood* so far. At any given point—isn't it amazing?—we can create a new narrative. We are not victims of our days. It doesn't matter where we've come from or what we think we've missed out on, we can change the story through traditions. We just have to keep our memory-making eyes open.

THINGS TO CONSIDER

As you brainstorm your own family traditions, here are some things to consider:

- What crazy, out-of-the-box memories from your childhood do you treasure most?
- Is it hard or easy for you to pop everyone in the car for a spontaneous adventure?
- What is your "default" personality, and what could you do that's a little different from that to surprise or entertain your kids?

- Thinking of your particular kids and their own personalities, what is one new adventure they would all enjoy?
- Looking back on your years as a memory-making parent or grandparent so far, in what ways do you wish you could "rewrite the story"?

SUGGESTED THINGS TO DO

- Take your kids to a new, fun place *just because.*
- Have a family day every year where you try something you've never done before.
- Together with your family, make a bucket list of things you want to do this season.
- Do something childish with your kids that you've never done before.
- Consider the bummin'-it adventure—the ultimate cheap outing: Pick up a bag of bread, meat, and cheese and drive till you see an area you like. Find a creek with a large rock or some unique place where you can sit and eat lunch. Simple, sometimes dangerous, magical, and memorable.[5]

CHAPTER 4

BEAUTY

On Teapots, Birdwatching, and the Smell of Bacon

*What greater joy can there be than to create a
holding place for all that is sacred in life: faith,
love, God, purpose, beauty, relationships, creativity,
fun, the art of life, safety, shelter, feasting?*

—SALLY CLARKSON[1]

DURING MY JUNIOR YEAR IN COLLEGE, I WENT
through a rather comical cowgirl stage. I plastered my walls with
pictures of ranches and cowboys. I wore tasseled earrings, stomped
around in a pair of cowboy boots, and booked a ticket out West
to work at a Young Life camp in Colorado for the summer. On
my application I listed "horse wrangler" as my job preference,
for obvious reasons. Never mind that I had ridden only half a
dozen times and was actually allergic to horses. Cowgirl life or
bust! In a stroke of what was probably divine providence, I was

placed in the next best option: camp baker—in a stuffy, over-heated kitchen.

My visions of leading trail riders on their horses across wild-flower fields while riding on my own trusty steed were replaced with 5:00 a.m. alarms. My days consisted of pounding hundreds of loaves of pizza dough or stirring chocolate chip banana loaf batter in a massive mixer for five hundred hungry campers. It was sweaty, tiring, mundane work that felt, honestly, disappointingly domestic for a Wild Cowgirl like me.

But in the afternoons, when we pulled off our hairnets and wiped the flour from our aprons, I would step into my tennis shoes . . . and run.

I would jog down the dusty drive that led to the camp, past the horse fields and trails and all up and down those curvy mountain roads. If I peered over the ledge, I'd see little mountain towns and a few winding rivers. And if I looked up? It was Colorado's majestic mountain peaks for days. After my run I'd sit at a little overlook near the camp. I'd pull my legs to my knees, gazing out over the heights, thinking, *I will always live near these mountains. I must make a promise to myself that I will always live near the mountains.*

Spoiler alert. The tasseled earrings broke, my cowboy boots got dusty, and Real Life interrupted, as it tends to do. And here I am, 2,032 miles from my precious mountains. I have never been back. Don't get me wrong: I love my Southern home, but I am a little sad I didn't keep that promise to myself. Twenty years later I've walked down the aisle and nursed three babies, and I *still* remember the life those Colorado mountains breathed into me.

Beauty changes us.

Beauty changes us.

As you think about which traditions you'll choose for your family, remember this: some of the most powerful traditions we can create are when we experience beauty together.

BEAUTY TRADITIONS INSIDE THE HOME

It might seem weird to start with interior design. After all, the word *beauty* probably conjures up visions of mountains, skies, and waterfalls. But let me ask you a question: How many hours a week do you spend gazing at waterfalls and fields of wildflowers? If you are like me, the answer is about zero hours. Now, a second question: How often do your eyes land on your living room coffee table? Yeah, I thought so. In the stage of child-rearing, entrenched in domestic life for better or for worse, we must work to bring beauty inside, as well as out.

For the Women Who Hate Their Homes

For about five years, I hated our home. Not the actual house, mind you, which had everything we needed, but the way it felt inside. Huge, dark, lumbering bookshelves towered over us in the living room, filled haphazardly with cheap plastic toys and ripped books. The walls in the entire house were dark gold (a curious decision by the previous owner), and the carpet was crusted and hopelessly stained. Everywhere my eyes fell, there was junk that I didn't need or love. For a literal five years, I did not put a single picture on a wall because I was afraid to make nail holes in paint I hated. (I know; it makes no sense.)

And in some weird way, it felt wiser or more frugal to leave it ugly, instead of "wasting" our money to make a beautiful home. I'd think, *Why should we spend money on paint and pillows?* After all, we had a house. *We had a house.* We had plenty of space, a nice yard, every appliance we'd want. So much of the world has nothing; I should be grateful. Occasionally I would get an inkling to replace the thrice-painted, clumsy black dressers my husband had owned since sixth grade, and I'd think, *I shouldn't spend money on new furniture. I should be grateful.*

But I didn't feel grateful; I felt depressed. It was like my blank gold walls were shouting at me, "You're a failure! You're bad at decorating!" The stained carpets would say, "You're a mess! You need to be cleaner!" And then sometimes I'd sit in my totally blank bedroom, and the angst would just wash over me. I couldn't articulate it, but my surroundings were affecting me in a profound way. I didn't like being in my house. It didn't matter how much I tried to convince myself that it didn't matter what it looked like; it bothered me.

But I didn't realize how much my kids were affected by our home as well. One night I was putting my almost-three-year-old to bed, and he looked up at his (of course, blank) walls above his head. "Mom, we need some pictures of some trucks up here . . . right here, over my head. I want two pictures of trucks and some blue on the walls and one, two, three lines of trucks . . ." In his sweet, two-year-old way, he longed for his version of beauty too.

The Home That Changed My Home

One fall, my friend Page moved into the home across the street. I walked in to borrow a can of beans one day and found her relaxing on a crisp white bedspread, in a clean bedroom, reading a magazine. I was stunned. It was all so beautiful and peaceful. I wanted to stay! Our bedroom never felt inviting. I always kind of wanted to escape it as soon as I could.

I left feeling something powerful; it was a different sensation from envy. As much as I had told myself the way my house looked didn't matter, I could not deny the effect Page's home had on me. I felt . . . *ministered to*. The walls are a beautiful, peaceful gray. (Benjamin Moore's Stonington Gray, to be exact; I know, because I later copied it for my own house.) There are plumpy white and gray chairs in the front room with baskets of books—from winsome picture books to beautiful devotionals. On the walls are all sorts of

Scripture artwork prints, Bible verse calligraphy, and framed family pictures. There are plush blankets and squishy pillows on the couch. And I also noticed it was clean. It looked lived-in, for sure. With four kids how could it not? But I noted a definite absence of dust bunnies in corners or mounds of junk mail on the counters.

It was a fact I could no longer avoid: *our home was missing beauty.*

"Home design really matters," says Design Mom blogger Gabrielle Blair. "It's the backdrop of our childhood. It helps tell our story and form our most precious memories. A well-designed home is one of the best gifts we can give our family."[2]

Money? No Money? Doesn't Matter

I want to make an important point here. *Creating beauty in your home does not take a lot of money.* I have been in homes elaborate and stuffy, which I wanted to leave as quickly as possible. Conversely, many quaint and simple homes are absolutely inviting. Take an example from Laura Ingalls Wilder's Little House series. Laura recalls their cozy, beautiful home: the way her mother smoothed out their checkered tablecloth, their three decorations above the door on the shelf that Pa made. The cleanliness of the regularly swept dirt floor. Laura took pride in their rustic, simple home, and it was beautiful. She treasured memories of the rocking chair by the sparkling fire, the table full of food and decorated for Christmas, the neatly made beds with straw-filled mattresses.

Rest assured, a beautiful home is absolutely within your reach on any budget. In my favorite book on home decorating, *The Nesting Place*, author Myquillyn Smith reminds us in her subtitle, "It doesn't have to be perfect to be beautiful."[3]

No, this is not a plug for consignment or yard sale scavenging, which I recognize can be wonderful if you are one of those blessed with thrift-store wizardry. Alas, for many of us, DIYing can feel as unnatural and daunting as ordering a tuna melt in a different language. If you are hopelessly horrible at finding diamonds in the rough on a budget, you can still have a home that makes you happy. No one has ever accused me of being a home decorating expert, but I used to have a home I hated. Now I have a home I love. So maybe I can share a few things about how to get from one home style to the other.

That Unavoidable "D" Word

Ah, yes. *Decluttering.* This step, unfortunately, isn't a little afternoon project, unless you're a minimalist by nature. In which case, I am very jealous of you already. I spent more than a year going through my house room by room, trashing or donating everything we'd accumulated over the last decade that I was staring at, tripping over, bumping into, and getting annoyed by. Little knickknacks I didn't like. Happy Meal trinkets that no one played with. Books we didn't read (or want to read). Clothes I hadn't worn since college. In her fabulous book *Decluttering at the Speed of Life*, Dana White notes, "As I got rid of obviously worthless stuff, I started realizing I loved something else. I loved space."[4] *Amen to that.*

Add Only What You Love

When I was sixteen, I was browsing in Pier 1 with my cousin. I found the most beautiful silver vase with pink-tinged white roses. It was around thirty dollars—a rather large chunk of change for a jobless teenager. I remember hesitating: *Should I buy this? Do I really need it?* And my cousin's words, still etched in my mind, "If you like it, you'll always have a place for it." She has a touch of prophecy; this sweet little vase I have gently unpacked into dorm rooms, moved from room to room in every home we have owned, and every time my eyes rest on it, I feel joy. Today part of the vase is chipped (boys), and one of the flowers loose (boys again). But it remains. It makes me happy. My goal is to make a practice of filling my home with these kinds of mementos.

Why am I talking about decorating homes? What does this have to do with traditions? You see, beauty inside the home becomes in its own right a sort of tradition, because our homes themselves form memories for our children. Remember: You choose strategically what enters your home. Things are memories too.

Things Are Traditions Too

I vividly remember the framed cross-stitching that read, "Unless the Lord builds the house, They labor in vain who build it," which forever hung in my childhood bathroom.[5] In my earliest years I could make sense only of the picture of the red house. I gradually got the idea that it was a Bible verse, but for the longest time I had no idea what *labor* or *vain* meant. I was probably in my teens before I finally pieced together the meaning of that verse: your plans will work only if God is working in them.

I read an interesting article that stated that Gen Xers and millennials no longer value the antiques passed down from their parents and grandparents.[6] While I don't think we are obligated to display Grandpa's two-hundred-piece train collection if we do not have room for it, I do think we should consider the value of pieces that have been handed to us by former generations. When we use Grandma's gravy boat, Mom's hand-sewn quilt, the candy bowl from Grandma's Grandma, we are honoring the memory of our loved ones and connecting our children's stories with their stories. These items are traditions, keeping the memory of something meaningful alive. When we choose beautiful or meaningful things for our home, we are choosing good traditions.

When you cast your eyes around your home, what do you see? What will your children remember? Will your kids have memories of counters full of junk, unpacked boxes lining the walls, plastic containers to step over in the living room? Or are there inviting reading spaces where the sun pours in from the windows? Comforting pillows to sink down in when your load is heavy? Fuzzy warm blankets to wrap around you when you read or watch a movie? Beautiful pictures or calligraphy on the walls to inspire? We need more of that.

I know that for every person reading this, there is a different perspective on what makes a home beautiful. I have my own ideas, and you have yours. Some of us are minimalists; some of us prefer a little "country clutter." Some of us can't stand dust on the tables, and others, it doesn't bother. Beauty looks different to each of us. *But it should be a goal.* It should be a home *you* love. And another thing: we should take our family's personalities and likings into consideration as we home-make. If you have a child who thrives in organized surroundings, at the very least, he or she should be allowed a personal space in which to retreat. Even better, try to keep the main living spaces as clear as you possibly can and keep the clutter out of sight. Similarly, if you're a minimalist, but you have a child who loves color and clutter and all the knickknacks, allow her personal space to splatter clutter to her heart's content.

ADDING BEAUTY TO OTHER TRADITIONS

Yes, we need beauty in our homes. But here's another thought: sometimes if a tradition isn't working or isn't fun, it's because it needs something beautiful added to it.

Let me give you an example. As a homeschooling mom, I'd heard a lot of chatter and raving about "morning time" for the homeschool day. I heard mamas gush about reading poetry, singing hymns, and having devotionals together. *I should do that*, I thought. So I bought all the right books, and every morning at 8:30 I barked orders for all the kids to gather around the table to start school. Guess what? It wasn't fun. We were doing all the right things, but none of us liked it. Don't tell the kids, but I always sort of dreaded the start of school myself. Secretly I'd linger over my breakfast and iPhone until the last possible moment when I knew we *had* to start.

About a year later I stumbled upon a homeschooling mom's fifteen-second video loop of their morning time. I watched this video obsessively. Seriously, it was almost unhealthy how many times I watched it. It made me cry, it made me think, it sent me to my knees. Everything about it was captivating and so different from us. They were drinking tea and eating something (muffins? biscuits? something delicious). They lit candles, they had little teacups and beautiful linens, and there was music and a big, inviting stack of books. They sat down and held hands and said their prayers, and the homeschool day began.

I could not stop thinking about this video. I got down on my knees, and I prayed something like this: "God, I know this woman is different from me. We aren't the same. But I feel like something's missing in what I'm doing. If there's something different you want *me* to do, please show me, and help me do it."[7]

It sounds crazy, but I literally spent the summer thinking and praying about this video. The whole thing was so winsome and so deliciously different from my Monday-morning marching orders for everyone to "Come to the table and be quiet!" By the time August rolled around, it was settled: school would be different. I bought a teapot, broke out my teacups, saucers, and sugar cubes, rounded up some candles and essential oils, and baked apple muffins.

And guess what? We all loved morning time. I was reading the same exact books; I was the same boring teacher who happens to also be their boring mom. But something—I couldn't put my finger on it—was different. I didn't have to nag the kids to come to start school. They raced in. One would eagerly place the teacups on saucers, one would pick the oils for the diffuser, one would light the candle.

One morning I snapped a picture of the morning scene: "This Is My Father's World" was streaming from the CD player, while the kids stirred sugar cubes into their tea, with the pleasant scent of the flowers, coconut candle, and lavender oil diffusing—the little hands hugging their curly white teacups—and it hit me.

Beauty.

The missing puzzle piece between this year and the last was beauty. We had the ritual down, but something had been missing. If you have some regular traditions that need improvement, consider this: maybe they need something extra delicious, or smelly, or with flower petals or soft, inviting fabric. Maybe you need some beauty. Here are a few other practical examples:

- Spice up family dinner with flowers and linens. Before you come to the table, wash up and dress in clean clothes.
- Have an elaborate Christmas dinner with candlesticks and Christmas decorations.
- Invest in beautiful seasonal decorations. My neighbor Alli is the best at this. She'll shop right after a holiday and grab some wonderful pieces at huge discounts. I still remember the feeling I'd get when my mom would wind lighted Christmas greenery down the banister in my childhood home. It was breathtaking.
- Gift your kids with a beautiful journal or Bible for their quiet times.

BEAUTY TRADITIONS OUTSIDE THE HOME

Do you have any traditions that involve the wonderful outdoors? Maybe it's chopping down a Christmas tree together, tromping the neighborhood after the first snowfall, an autumn hike, waking to watch the sunrise on your beach vacation, or planting a vegetable garden in spring. Chances are, you probably have some you don't even realize. Recognize them for what they are: traditions. Talk them up, relish them.

Celebrating Traditions in Nature

I'm a big fan of family hikes, whether at a local park or a mountain two hours away. For a period in our homeschool experience, we celebrated Friday afternoon adventures. As soon as naps were done, we would pack snacks and head to a local park. One time my five-year-old was nearly attacked by a very aggressive goose. Several times we got lost in the trails behind a park. (Note: for children younger than ten years old, this is to be read as *thrilling*.)

We're always on the lookout for interesting souvenirs to collect on our outings. (How many times have I accidentally smashed or trashed someone's very dear pinecone? *Sigh*.) One day I challenged the kids by saying, "Hey kids, let's try to find the most beautiful rock we can, and we'll bring it home and write the date and the name of the park on it." The kids loved this idea, and it has become somewhat of a family tradition. We have quite a smattering of rocks decorating the house now. In full disclosure, the same number of poor rocks probably hasn't survived to become members of the collection. Some have been stuck under car seats, left in backpacks, or washed in pants pockets. I am quite certain there are a few in our minivan cupholders as I type this. Nevertheless, our rock collection chronicles quite a journey—and a whole lot of memories to boot. We've retrieved some from the bases of waterfalls, from underneath boulders, from the feet of towering pines.

And then there was the time we scored the crowning glory, known as "the Smartt Family Rock." We were on the top of a mountain hike when my oldest son spotted a rock (maybe more aptly termed *boulder*) that inspired him. "Hey! This can be the Smartt Family Rock! Let's all take turns carrying it down the mountain!"

My husband and I looked at each other. We were already taking turns carrying things—a toddler, two backpacks, and some special feathers we had been ordered not to crush. But the kids' passion was contagious. If I tell you it weighed twenty-five pounds, I am not exaggerating. I put down the toddler to take the first leg of the journey. I felt it all; my back was aching, my wrists burning, fingers sweating. I couldn't drop it—it was the Smartt Family Rock! We had a mission, it was hard, and we carried the load together. I will not lie: my husband definitely carried this boulder for a good long chunk, and I found myself treasuring his steady, strong pace, his persevering, patient spirit. But we all helped, and it sits now on our hearth—an Ebenezer, a monument to our family, to our journey, and to adventures together.[8]

Simply getting outdoors regularly, whatever that looks like for you, is the beginning of wonderful nature traditions. Every season offers unique opportunities for traditions that honor the beauty to be found in nature.

Celebrating Beauty in Fall

I know you people love autumn because if I pop on social media in early October, my feed is blown up with artsy selfies of people holding pumpkin lattes and showing off their swanky new rain boots. Alas, I seem to be in the minority, mourning the loss of heat and suntans. But fall is a great time for traditions, isn't it?

My extended family has a tradition of going to the North Carolina mountains for a weekend every fall. Thirteen grandchildren, ten adults, and a lot of memories. There are long hikes, fishing, Nerf-gun battles, afternoons with marshmallows and a roaring fire, movie night, always beef stew and crusty rolls, and a special take-home craft. Here are more ideas for fall traditions:

- Drive through the mountains to look at the colorful leaves.
- Make a fall bucket list that includes things such as a mountain hike, apple and pumpkin picking, hayride, corn maze, and river fishing.
- Host a fall-themed neighborhood block party, like a chili cook-off.
- Make your own apple cider or apple pie.
- Read poems about fall.
- Make your own leaf rubbings.

Celebrating Beauty in Winter

There's nothing quite as wonderful as a day spent romping in the snow. If you live in the bitter-cold north, you're probably laughing hysterically. But truly, I think every child should have at least a few chances to enjoy snow. My in-laws live in a snowier area than we do, and I've ordered them to call us immediately if they're expecting a snowstorm so we can be storm chasers and spend a few days sledding.

Of course, winter can also be a bit bleak and positively unbeautiful. One way we have experienced beauty in the winter is to hang a bird feeder outside our breakfast nook. This has been no small thing for my children; it brings us such joy. One child printed a bird-identifying chart for our region and has become quite the little ornithologist (bird watcher, that is). My three-year-old loves to fill the bird feeder and to know that she is "giving the birdies lunch." We had a terrible time when the squirrels scavenged the birdseed, and that led to its own adventure. The boys would hover inside the patio door with their foam-bullet guns, ready to assail the woodsy thieves. Eventually we upgraded to a squirrel-proof bird feeder. What a hoot it was seeing these confounded squirrels attempt to get birdseed out of the squirrel-proof design. This entertained our family nearly every day for months.

Here are a few more winter traditions for your family to consider:

- Always enjoy chicken soup, shepherd's pie, or hot cocoa on the first snowfall.
- Wake your kids up when it starts snowing. (Except, of course, the babies. *Never* wake the babies!)
- Make a bird feeder (you knew it was coming) for your outdoor friends.
- Have a cozy movie night on a freezing evening.
- Read a book aloud by the fire.
- Have an indoor campout.

Celebrating Beauty in Spring

I am actually horrible at anything to do with dirt, which is comical because my husband works in the landscaping industry. I probably embarrass him with my black thumb. I sure do love the beauty of the flowers in the spring, though. In my childhood home, I'd watch for the daffodils to poke up as the weather warmed. I want to create these cozy nooks of flowery beauty in and around our home. Here are a few ideas for spring traditions:

- Plant a family garden. One year my kids grew tomatoes and set up a little stand by the side of the road to sell their harvest.
- Provide each child with a personal flowerpot where he or she can grow his or her own fruit or flower.
- Let your kids stomp in the rain—and maybe join them too.
- If you have little kids, do Easter egg hunts over and over in

the house and yard. They love it even if there's nothing in the eggs!

- Pull a chair to the window and watch a thunderstorm together.

Celebrating Beauty in Summer

There are few things I love more than a good summer bike ride. During our college years, my sister and I would bike around our neighborhood after sunset. I love the feeling of the wind through my hair, the breeze cooling the mild sweat I've started to break, and the beauty of pushing so hard up a hill, then gliding freely all the way down the other side.

As a mom, I've tried to incorporate this favorite pastime with our family. For a while it meant pulling a giant double-seater cart behind my bike, which made me feel (and look) like an overworked pack mule. Lest you are tempted to think I am in incredible physical shape, I must clarify that these treks often made me feel as if I were going to pass into the other life. I usually had to stop and manually pull the cart up big hills. It's not always idyllic. Sometimes it involves getting off your bike to encourage someone to make it up a hill, fielding questions about squirrel eating habits when you're huffing and puffing, or booking it home in a thunderstorm. But these are all treasured memories.

And camping! Incidentally, I loathe camping if tents are involved. Our marriage survived the experience once, barely. But RV camping—that's a whole new world. The first night in our (rented) RV, we sat on camp chairs while our kids poked around in the fire and ate popcorn. We looked at each other and said, "This is amazing." Now, we have a family goal to travel from our East Coast home to the Grand Canyon in an RV. I know for many families the camping season is a most treasured tradition.

Maybe biking and camping aren't your favorites. Are you a waterfall-mountain-hiking sort of person? A lake lover? Fishing, gardening, surfing, golfing, front-porch-swinging, boating, evening-strolling, tennis, or classical-music-on-the-lawn lover? What makes *your* heart skip a beat? What would your family love most? Here are a few specific suggestions for awesome summer traditions:

- Celebrate National Donut Day on the first Friday in June.
- Visit a hot air balloon festival.
- Go tech-free for one week. (You may be surprised how much you all enjoy this one.)
- Celebrate National Ice Cream Day on the third Sunday in July with homemade ice cream or a trip to a local shop.
- Have a low-country boil and eat outdoors. (This summer one-pot meal of shrimp, sausage, corn, and potatoes is famous in the low country of Georgia and South Carolina.)

THE POWER OF SMELL

My brother says, "They should make a perfume of bacon. That's what guys would really like." I can neither deny nor confirm whether bacon perfume would be a success, but I do consider the sense of smell to be greatly overlooked.

Smells are powerful. Sometimes when company was coming, my mom would put a pot of water on the stove and simmer cinnamon sticks. I do that every so often and think back to our Brantwood Drive childhood home. Whenever I'm baking with vanilla, I call over the nearest child to catch a whiff from the bottle. I wonder if they'll think of me when they smell vanilla? As I write this, essential oils are the thing. I don't know, as this book gathers dust on the shelves, if essential oils will be relegated to the past alongside stuff like margarine and Chia pets. I sure hope not. I love diffusing lavender at bedtime, a Christmas blend during the holidays, and an immune-boosting blend when we're sick. These smells will help to make memories for our kids.

THE POWER OF MUSIC

Back when I was in the thick of diaper changing and toddler tantrums, I would sometimes call my mom around 4:00 or 5:00 p.m.—internationally recognized by moms as the Worst Hour of the Day—with a crack in my voice and tears in my eyes. I was exhausted, the kids were exhausted; tensions were high everywhere. She would say, "You should put on some music, Jessica. They say, 'Music calms the savage beasts!'"[9]

I often forget about the power of music. Where's your phone right now? Likely within arm's reach, right? In it you have free access to the most amazing musical performances of all time. We simply have to think of it.

Music can be powerful to a child, and it doesn't have to be kid's music. I spent a lot of time as a child on my grandparents' horse farm. After twelve hours of climbing trees, building forts, and playing flashlight tag (we had terribly deprived childhoods without all the technology, you see), we'd gather after dark in my uncle Stevie's house. Uncle Stevie played the guitar and sang, Uncle Danny played the bass, cousin Charlie played the drums, Aunt Rebecca sang, and Aunt Marci danced. Boy could she dance—for a mom. Some lucky kid got the egg shaker, and we played old folk and country songs for hours. We didn't know all the words, but we smiled the entire time.

BEAUTY IN THE EYE OF THE BEHOLDER

We've always loved nature walks. There are so many exciting discoveries for kids: birds, giant locusts, squishy (or squashed) worms, a family of bunnies, walking sticks, and interesting leaves. The key is not to hurry, which is harder for moms than kids, and to keep your eyes open for treasures. Maybe an older child will have tastes in music or decorating that we don't share quite so much. This may be a good time to remind ourselves that beauty, after all, is in the eye of the beholder. At one point I had one sweet little guy who was adamant about stopping on our walks to admire every sewage drainpipe, garbage truck, and street sweeper. This, to him, was beauty. I finally learned to stop redirecting him, and we gushed over the drainpipes together.

THINGS TO CONSIDER

As you brainstorm your own family traditions, here are some things to consider:

- Can you think of someone's home that you would describe as warm and beautiful? What makes it so?
- What's a treasured memory you have involving nature?
- What's a state, city, or area where you'd love to travel?
- How did music play a role in your childhood?
- What are your favorite smells?
- What's your favorite season to spend outside?

SUGGESTED THINGS TO DO

- Decide on two things you will do to bring beauty inside your home.
- Make a bucket list of beautiful natural places you want to visit with your family.

- Brainstorm one new way to enjoy each season.
- Consider purchasing a beautiful piece of artwork for your child as a birthday gift.
- Enjoy good music as a family and consider introducing your kids to some classical pieces. Three great ones to start with are "Simple Gifts" from *Appalachian Spring* by Aaron Copland, "The Lark Ascending" by Ralph Vaughan Williams, and "Canon in D" by Johann Pachelbel.

CHAPTER 5

FOOD

Memories That Stick to Your Ribs

This is a bleak, fallen old world. Life has real pain, disappointment, and evil. Whatever lies ahead, the best preparation is a childhood with a core of everyday calmness/well-being that is given substance by a cheerful, comforting, satisfying, and full-of-hope kitchen.

—SUSAN SCHAEFFER MACAULAY[1]

FOOD HAS MINISTERED TO ME MY ENTIRE LIFE. YOU know how every family has that one person who will always scarf down the leftovers? My family says, "Oh, give it to Jessica! She'll eat it!" It was kind of awkward with my husband and me at first because instead of having one of those dainty wives who shoved off her dinner after a few disinterested bites, I was the one eyeing his pizza crust and wondering if it was free game. My most common dinnertime reprimand as a child was "Jessica, please slow down. Your dinner is not going to get up and walk away."

Because of this deep, lifelong affinity between me and food, I am a good one to speak to the power of food traditions. Food and I are tight. Food speaks to me. It is my love language, my passion, a balm to my soul.

THE POWER OF FOOD

It is hard to quantify the times God has used food to minister to me. From Mom's chicken casserole with the swirly egg noodles and breadcrumb topping that I requested every birthday, to the time my cousin baked my sixteenth birthday cake in the spitting image of a lamb, to the amazing postpartum meals I received from friends—there are just too many stories to list.

I'm not trying to be dramatic. I think there is a significant point here. We often relegate food hospitality to the stuff that doesn't matter quite as much as other spiritual acts of service. I am telling you satisfying food, served with beauty, can change people.

Recently I asked my family, "How has food been meaningful to you?" Do this sometime; it is a powerful thing. My brothers-in-law, grown men with tattoos and scruffy beards, brimmed with emotion remembering Christmas brunch, Sunday lunch with Grandpa at the local pancake house, donuts and hot dogs every night at the fair. My eighty-nine-year-old Grammy's face spread into a wistful, teary smile when she recalled cinnamon roll-making day from her childhood. Food is more than food. I know this, too, as one who has shed tears in the line of a breakfast buffet.

A few years ago my husband and I celebrated our anniversary with a weekend at the beautiful Grove Park Inn and Resort in the mountains of North Carolina. For my part, this getaway could not have come at a more ideal time. I was at a very low point. I was physically and emotionally depleted. My anxieties were raging. I felt disappointed in myself for the way the last school year had gone, and I was convinced that I was a failure as a homeschool mother. I had to resign from a position I had enjoyed at my church because I was so overwhelmed, and that felt embarrassing. Most important, I was exhausted in every sense of the word. I wanted to sleep all day long. My soul was craving rest on a deep, visceral level.

A weekend away with Todd was a balm to my soul. We hiked, swam, and (best of all) spent large amounts of time doing absolutely nothing. The whole experience was one of the best trips either of us had ever taken. But on to the important part: the food.

Our second day there, we took the elevator to one of the resort's restaurants for the breakfast buffet. We sat down to steaming cups of coffee overlooking the mountains, then walked up to the serving line to fill our plates. I looked at the bountiful displays of delicious gourmet food—from perfectly cooked hash brown potatoes, to the best cheese grits I had ever tasted, a homemade juice bar, freshly baked fruit pastries, crisp brown-sugar bacon. I am not lying to you when I say tears sprang to my eyes. All the beauty of the weekend came to a head in that one moment of realizing *this*. This is a gift from God. The rest, beauty, and nourishment your soul needs—He is providing it.

It may sound totally dramatic to say that hash browns in a breakfast buffet line brought me to tears. But, seriously, they were so good. My guess is that if you, too, have experienced years of eating cold scrambled egg breakfasts in five-minute intervals while stopping to wipe someone's bottom, break up a fight, and unload the dishwasher, then perhaps you can identify with my exultation at someone else serving me such a divine breakfast.

I think it's interesting that God made eating such a diverse, full experience. I hate to be crude, but He could have made the food go in the same way it comes out. Bland, routine, unsophisticated, sufficient, private. Instead, it is an experience involving all of the senses and textures in life—from the fluffy lightness of a hot baked potato to rich chewy shreds of beef, from juicy cold watermelon to warm crusty bread.

Food has great power to heal, to minister, to love, and to create memories that last.

> Food has great power to heal, to minister, to love, and to create memories that last.

As mothers, we know this is a convenient fact because we have more than one thousand opportunities every year to serve up love and memories around the table. In a childhood, this tops off at nearly twenty thousand meals. If your children are like mine and actually require sustenance every twenty-seven minutes they are awake, then the opportunities for bonding over food become exactly . . . infinite.

THE PROBLEM OF MOMS AND THE MINISTRY OF FOOD

There is this disconnect in me, though. I have received grace at the table. Good food makes me feel loved. But it has taken me quite some time to reciprocate the same level of blessing to my own nuclear family. I have friends who have remained gourmet through the diaper years, roasting brussels sprouts and toasting crostini even while the masses tug at their yoga-pants legs and demand more Cheerios.

I am not one of these women. Motherhood undid me.

I lived in a shade of survival mode for what felt like a decade. I felt like I was winning if I simply *made dinner*. This was not the time for culinary experiments. A meat, a starch, and a vegetable—we lived in sufficiency. Why waste edible adventures on toddlers? I had one child who determined pie crust was the literal devil. How can one reason with such nonsense? And lastly, I had real limits in the kitchen. Some weeks we had something like negative twenty dollars to spend on food. I couldn't afford to experiment. Seriously, what kind of mothers are actually making recipes with currants? As if all of these were not obstacles enough, we have food allergies to deal with. My list of delicious and also safe meals was painfully short. At dinnertime, we were just surviving.

If you are like me, most mealtimes with your children don't seem memorable or winsome. In fact, if you have a child below the age of six, chances are these mealtime moments are even quite stressful. You have one child who talks incessantly about football. One has suddenly developed a horrific aversion to zucchini. Another is violently scattering muffin crumbs in a five-yard radius around the table. By the time you've redirected child number one away from the New York Giants and back to the zucchini, exchanged a "bad fork" for a good one, and cleaned up the juice someone spilled into the cracks of the kitchen table, your own pasta is colder and even more unappetizing than it was originally. Yes, food in motherhood is a mixed bag. While we (and our children, I would argue) stand to benefit *especially* from food's comforts and pleasures during this season of life, it is even that much harder to perform the miracle that is dinner.

Designer, mom, and entrepreneur Joanna Gaines describes it perfectly: "Sometimes cooking can feel like work after an already long workday. Or I imagine the cleanup and wonder if it's really worth it. But once I tune in to the fact that my family receives my cooking for them as an act of love—that it's actually something that makes them feel cared for—it shifts my entire perspective . . . The chore I dreaded for so long, I have come to find out is actually a gift."[2]

It is easy to lose sight of the fact that food can be—and

is—ministry to our families. My goal in this chapter is to offer specific suggestions to make food traditions memorable yet doable.

THE GIFT OF TAKE-OUT FOOD TRADITIONS

Let's begin by recognizing the fact that you can create treasured food traditions *without cooking anything.* And all the moms and dads said, "Amen." Yes, it is true; there can be many beautiful, precious family memories involving takeout, restaurants, and all sorts of experiences when you did not prepare the food. Now, isn't that exciting?!

Here's a great example. My brother John has a personal goal to sample all the donut bakeries within fifty miles of his home. (Let's give credit where credit is due: he has nearly achieved his goal.) I'm sure his little ones will remember Saturday mornings driving to the next town over for the latest take on a strawberry jam-filled fluffy pastry. Another sweet twist to this tradition: he often drops one off for my son, as he knows he absolutely loves donuts. They have a special donut-shaped aspect to their relationship.

Here's one from my own childhood. This one is going to appall the real foodies because it involves the one and only McDonald's fast food restaurant. When I was in sixth grade, I had to attend First Communion class at our church. The classes were held in the evenings, which meant that my mom had to drive me downtown, after dark, after getting the other kids in bed. I realize now this was no easy feat for her.

Although I greatly appreciate the sacrament of Holy Communion, I have to confess that I don't remember too much of the theology I learned in those weekly evening classes. Do you know what I do remember? *McDonald's cheeseburgers.* We'd leave First Communion class, and my mom would steer us toward the drive-thru of the golden arches to order me the rarest of treats: a cheeseburger, small fries, and an icy Coke. (I have always loved my second dinners.) If I try hard enough, I can remember the crinkly unfolding of the paper and the warm, oozing cheese on that mouthwatering sandwich. Remembering this special ritual still warms my heart. It was just me and Mom. And the cheeseburgers. She could have easily skipped it; it was late, and surely she was exhausted. But it was a special ritual that she knew I would love. I asked her recently about this tradition, and who knew? Her own mom took her to McDonald's after her Communion class.

You don't have to sweat in a kitchen to make these kinds of memories. You don't have to crack open a cookbook, knead dough, or wash a single pan. But with some thoughtfulness, some consistency, and some intention, it becomes a treasured memory. Isn't that a relief?

THE GIFT OF *EVERYDAY* FAMILY MEALS

Of course, a childhood of only McDonald's cheeseburgers or fast-food breakfast sandwiches would be really sad. (Not to mention unhealthy.) And this is where our second example comes in: the comfort of regular meals. These "staple" meals that your family loves are anchors, memories, ministry. Mom's chicken noodle soup, Dad's chicken hot off the grill, steamy tortilla soup on wintry nights: these casual, normal, nothing-special meals will be the meals your children will ask for when they are home from college, the ones they long for when they're sick, the ones they will attempt to reproduce in apartments with their new spouses.

Let's think for a moment about dinnertime decorum. We have already acknowledged the fact that dinnertime with small children is basically a circus. This is true. But it's just a fact that chicken casserole, warmed over in the microwave and eaten alone in front of an iPad at a side table is not going to have the same nostalgic charm ten years later as it will if you eat together. Meals require community. They require us to sit down together—smashed green beans, tantrums, picky eaters, and all.

Jesus knew it. On His last evening with His disciples, He didn't take them to the temple to squeeze in one last reading of the Torah. He didn't do one final whirlwind miracle healing tour. *No, on Jesus' last evening with His friends, they ate dinner.* A reclining, savoring sort of dinner (Luke 22:7–39).

Have you ever observed the magic that food works in a group of people? As we sip, savor, sample, and are satisfied, the mood changes. Food makes people happy, and happy people bond. I admit I can be a bit of a tyrant when it comes to observing family dinner at the table. ("I don't care if the game went into overtime; *it's dinnertime, and you'll come right this second!*") But it is important for me to remember that while half the battle is getting the troops rounded up to eat together at the table, the atmosphere matters greatly. Meals together should be pleasant. Whatever wrongs have been committed beforehand should be shut out. When we bow our heads, we take a collective deep breath and start over.

When I was little, sometimes my mom would sit silently before she said the prayer, with a pensive, help-me-Jesus sort of pause. I always thought it was kind of odd. What in the world could she be thinking of? (I know now.) We parents have the power to rewrite the story at the table, to set a different tone. If you are like me, flipping the switch from a "momster" commandeering the unruly troops to a warm and inviting dinnertime host is not going to happen easily. But it is the goal.

The point of what I am saying here is this: we do not often give the kitchen table enough credit. Sometimes in my mind, feeding my family is a task on the same level as scrubbing the inside of the toilet bowl: uninspiring, mandatory, necessary.

Dinner is not like this. It is different. By faithfully cooking nourishing foods and gathering together to enjoy them, we are creating memories and building a wall of character and love one brick at a time. Let us not become weary in making nutritious meals and eating them together, for twenty years later we may reap a beautiful harvest if we do not give up.

THE GIFT OF *SPECIAL* FAMILY MEALS

Let's take it up a level and talk about special family dinners. You may be thinking, *What's the point of that? My kids are little, picky, and rowdy. Do I really need to go through the effort to make certain meals extra special?* Trust me, I understand that concern.

Recently I was listening to a podcast interview with the mom of a very large family. This mom was talking about her dinnertime logistics, and she said something to the effect of, "Dinner doesn't have to be anything special. It doesn't matter if it's canned soup or tuna sandwiches—my kids will eat anything happily." While I understand the point she was making (we don't have to overthink dinner), something about her comment didn't sit well with me. I let it simmer a few weeks and then came to a conclusion: Yes, kids can be happy with anything. But I have also seen tremendous fruit in my life from investing time, energy, and money into making dinner extravagant.

Extravagant is a comical word to hear from someone who spent five years literally making the same twelve meals for dinner. Yes, for the first five years of motherhood, I was simply surviving in the kitchen. The bulk of our weekday dinners were bland and predictable, chaotic mealtimes that I managed mainly on my own due to my husband's work hours.

I can thank my friend Carey for my change of heart. It was

just a passing phrase she used, but it changed everything. She was telling me about their dinnertime conversation games, and she said, "Oh, we don't do that every night. Just on family dinner night."

That little phrase literally changed the course of our family meals. I had assumed people were either family-dinner people or not. I assumed there were those people who went all out for dinner, and those who did not. And we, with our turkey burgers, frozen fries, carrot sticks, and paper-towel napkins, were quite clearly the nots.

But as she talked, I realized that we could do a special family dinner *sometimes*, at least one night a week. No, it wouldn't be perfect, but it would be something. It would be a start.

How to Create a Family Dinner Night

From day one, family dinner night has been an absolute success. Here are the rules so you can create one too.

Designate a night.

We chose Thursday, but if we can't do that, we pick a different night. When you have kids with sports seasons or scout meetings, you may need to change your night for a season, and that's okay. The point is to pick a specific time and guard it as much as you reasonably can.

Create ambiance.

This is oh-so-crucial. I went to a discount home store and bought a crisp gray tablecloth and new, yet-to-be-stained white cotton napkins. I journeyed to the nether regions of our cabinets to retrieve my fine wedding china. (Because if these precious people aren't worth it, who in the world is?) I bought some white pillar candles and short, sparkling crystal candle holders. And always flowers, even if I have to clip them off the bushes in the front yard and stick them in a glass cup. You may be surprised how simple decor changes can change the dinner mood entirely.

Choose yummy food.

Hear me out: there is nothing wrong with food that gets the job done. I'm not here to hate on tacos, spaghetti, meatloaf, or whatever those staple weekday meals are in your home that may elicit groans or frowns while steadfastly nourishing your people week after week. But family dinner is not the night for these. Be extravagant. *Make it yummy!* A few meals in our family dinner rotation include pot roast and homemade applesauce, fried chicken, California BLT sandwiches and homemade steak fries, BBQ chicken with all the fixings, and beef stew.

And dessert!

I rarely make dessert, so it's a special treat on Thursdays when we have a special homemade dessert. Whether it's homemade chocolate chip cookies, an apple pie, berry cobbler, or even a giant fruit salad (which is a huge hit in our family), dessert is a nonnegotiable on family dinner night.

Serve willingly.

Family dinner is one of our favorite traditions. But! *It is a lot of work.* There are some Thursday afternoons when I face a mounting to-do list: bake homemade cobbler, roast a chicken, brown a gravy, do the dishes, iron the tablecloth. Sometimes it is the last thing I feel like doing. There will be many times that it is difficult, and you will be tempted to give up. I have a few words of advice.

First of all, I pray for strength. I know praying for strength to get the potatoes mashed may not feel as noble as praying for holiness or hurricane disaster victims or those sorts of things. But I ask the Lord for help to do this worthy thing, and He always provides. Second, I remind myself of what I am accomplishing. In order for there to be a nest, there must be a nestmaker.[3] I am making a fine nest.

Oh yes, there have been many, many times when family dinner involves a personal sacrifice of my time, patience, and energy. It is 5:45 p.m., I'm scrambling to get the chicken breaded and coated, my toddler is having a breakdown because she didn't get a good nap, and all of a sudden it feels like it's 500 degrees in my kitchen. Suddenly, instead of having cozy, maternal feelings toward the members of my family, I begin to feel more of a rage that things are so difficult and wonder why in the world we have family dinner anyway because it is absolutely not worth the effort.

And then we sit down.

I have never regretted making family dinner a tradition. Not one time.

Going Deeper

There is something else too. I'm going a little deep here, so if you're starting to get especially cozy and drift off, come back to this section after you brew a cup of coffee. *I have realized that family dinner has worked on me, on my heart, in a way I didn't expect.* The concept of family dinner has reworked my preconceptions about what is an important use of my time. Time is the great commodity for modern individuals such as me. We are fed the lie that we deserve to be important. Important people spend their time bettering themselves—toning their calf muscles, practicing for their next triathlon, building their platform and pet projects, refilling their manicures, getting social media likes, and updating their wardrobes.

Ironing a napkin does none of this. It's a waste of time. Yet is it? "Feasting is not only a way to meet physical and emotional needs. It's also a powerful tool for making disciples."[4] Dare to waste your time on your family.

MORE WEEKLY MEAL TRADITIONS

What if you agree that family dinner is worth it, but your schedule is so super packed that it is not actually a possibility? I'm not there yet, but I've heard that the teenage years (otherwise known as the Era Spent in the Car) become absolutely cram-packed with events.

A good friend of mine said her parents faced this dilemma and devised a creative solution. With five older children, the family was simply too busy to do a regular dinner together. Not to be deterred, they began a new tradition: family breakfast. Every weekday morning, Mrs. Wray made a delicious hot breakfast. And it didn't end there. One family member was assigned to bring a joke, one to prepare a devotional. Mr. Wray would read the Bible, and Mrs. Wray would review some Latin roots. It was a fun, memorable tradition that met the challenges of busy, modern-day parenting head-on.[5] I love this creativity and determination to be innovative about family mealtime.

While this solution certainly did require some effort, I am sometimes amazed at how simple family mealtime really is, in its essence. As it turns out, there is nothing intrinsically complex about making pot roast (or pancakes) and sitting down with the people you live with for twenty-five minutes. The hardest part is the decision to do it. You must accept that the effort is more valuable in the long run than time you could be spending otherwise.

Here are a few weekly meal traditions you can consider:

- One night per week when one child, or all of them, makes dinner for the family.
- Saturday special breakfast, whether it's donuts from a local shop or homemade pancakes.
- Sunday snack dinner! Make it easy on Mom. Serve snack foods, such as cheese, bread, fruit, nuts, and vegetables. This is one of my family's favorite traditions.
- Choose one day a week to make a special treat or dessert, like homemade cookies, bread, or a favorite dessert with dinner.

THE MINISTRY OF SPECIAL-OCCASION FOODS

We've established that creating food memories can be as easy as a favorite take-out tradition. We've discussed the power of predictable weekday meals, and we made the case for a special weekly family dinner.

There's another category of food memories, and it will perhaps be the one your kids remember the most. In fact, it's probably the one you remember the most from your own childhood. These are the extravagant, over-the-top feasts or special occasion meals. The not-everyday dinners. The New Year's Eve pot roast dinner, the legendary strawberry Jell-O birthday cake, or the special cinnamon rolls on Christmas. My goal is to remind you exactly how powerful these celebrations can be, to keep you doing the ones you are doing, and to prompt you to add a few more. These are the crowning glories of food experiences.

When I was engaged to be married, my mom and sisters threw me a bridal shower. I think it was the best day of my life. I spent an embarrassing amount of time primping and dressing before this event. (Because I had no children and was newly engaged and had absolutely unholy amounts of time to spend on myself.) I had picked out the most beautiful flowy white dress with tiny blue and red flowers. I had adorable red wedge sandals and matching red pearl jewelry. All of the women I loved most would be in one room at one time. I would be getting gifts to use in my new home, with my new husband. Could my life actually be better? No. It could not.

My mom and sisters knew that food was my love language, so I would be enjoying all of my favorite foods at one time. When I walked into the brightly decorated kitchen, it was one of the most beautiful sights I had ever seen. On my mom's dining room table was the most succulent display of tasty comforts. Little tiny home-made cinnamon rolls, warm chicken biscuits, hot hash browns, little cupcakes with pastel blue frosting, a coffee and mimosa bar, brown-sugar bacon, and fresh blueberry, blackberry, and raspberry parfaits.

It was an extravagant, elaborate, overwhelming display of foods. When I saw the overflowing table, I felt so loved. I still treasure that morning. Now that I am on this side of parenthood, I realize how much work went into that morning. I realize that my mom brain-stormed that menu for months. She made to-do lists and shopping lists for weeks. It was a labor of love.

What are the special events from your life that you still remember, and how did food play a role in them? Do you treasure the memory of Grandma's homemade pasta? Your aunt's authentic empanadas? The Fourth of July flag cake? The Super Bowl cheese dip? Don't you doubt it for a second, mama: so many of the special food traditions you have started are way more treasured than you can imagine.

THE GIFT OF FAMILY TIME
IN THE KITCHEN

When I asked my brother-in-law John about his childhood memories involving food, he had story after story, recipe after recipe. Interestingly he said, "It's not just the food smells or eating it. *It's the prep work that we do*, like working together the night before for the Christmas breakfast."[6] I tend to think I need to do all the work for a special celebration myself. Not only should my family help as they are able, but this pitching in can actually become a treasured memory in and itself!

Oh-so-very-often as I am making dinner, I'll hear a stumble and bumble from the corner of the kitchen, and here comes my sweet toddler, dragging a giant chair over to my work station. She wants to help. I'll be the first to tell you this help is sometimes anything but that! But we are making more than dinner; we are making memories. My sister Jenny took the kids-in-the-kitchen idea a step further and instituted "Thursday takeover." Her kids pick the menu, help grocery shop, and cook the dinner from start to finish.

> We are making more than dinner; we are making memories.

My sister Julie is a wonderful chef and baker and loves spending time in the kitchen. She has many ideas for family culinary adventures. Here are a few:

- Make "bread in a bag." Lots of recipes for this are available online. It's a simple way for kids to prepare their own individual loaves of bread.
- Make "coffee mug" brownies. This is a cute and very adaptable recipe for an individual dessert.
- Have a pizza night and let each person make their own individual pizza.

- Have fondue night. Prep the materials together and enjoy dipping and tasting.

We've covered a lot of ground in this food chapter. We've talked about how family dinner can be hard, but both the weekly and special days are worth it. We've talked about easy food traditions and elaborate ones. I hope you have some new ideas for making memories in the kitchen.

THINGS TO CONSIDER

As you brainstorm your own family traditions, here are some things to consider:

- What are your favorite memories or traditions that involve food?
- What's your biggest challenge as a parent regarding family meals?
- Do you have any easy take-out or restaurant traditions in your family?
- Can you think of more ways to involve your kids in the kitchen?

SUGGESTED THINGS TO DO

- Ask your husband and kids what food traditions they love the most, and make sure they happen regularly.
- Have a restaurant night every so often. I fondly remember this tradition from my childhood; my mom would make a menu with choices, and we would get to pick our meal for

the evening. When I grew up, I realized the entree options for our restaurant were a weekly hodgepodge of leftovers that Mom was too frugal to scoop into the trash. And yet it was so magical to us! Eventually you can reverse it. When they're ready, let your kids be the chefs and waitresses of the restaurant for *you* sometime!

- Try adding a fancy family dinner (or breakfast) to your routine.
- Let the birthday child pick the meal!

RECISPES

Here are a few of our family's very favorite meals.

Favorite Family Dinner

STEAK COBB SALAD WITH HOMEMADE OVEN FRIES

This meal dirties a lot of dishes, but my family loves it. And it's (kinda) healthy! You can add or delete ingredients depending on your family's preferences.

INGREDIENTS
4 to 6 russet potatoes (or a package of frozen French fries)
6 tablespoons of liquified coconut oil or olive oil
1 to 2 sirloin steaks or your preferred cut for grilling
olive oil, for cooking steaks
romaine lettuce
cherry tomatoes, a few per person
4 hard-boiled eggs, chopped
6 slices bacon, cooked and chopped
cheddar cheese, optional
1 avocado, diced

INSTRUCTIONS
1. Cut russet potatoes into half-inch slices and then again to make into steak fries. Toss with the coconut oil (or olive oil) and sprinkle with salt. Lay flat on a baking sheet and bake at 425 degrees for 20 minutes, then flip them and cook for 20 more minutes or until desired level of crispness.
2. Salt and pepper the steaks. Heat enough olive oil in a pan to cook the steaks on the stovetop. When the oil starts smoking, add steak (one at a time, if necessary) and cook on each side

for 4 to 7 minutes, depending on your preference for doneness. Rest for 5 minutes, then slice diagonally or cube.

3. Layer romaine lettuce, cherry tomatoes, hard-boiled eggs, bacon, cheddar cheese, avocado, steak, and fries. Top with your favorite dressing and season with salt and pepper.

Favorite Family Dessert
BERRY CRUMBLE

This is especially delicious served warm and topped with whipped cream or ice cream. Delicious in any season!

INGREDIENTS
1/4 cup coconut oil or butter, plus extra for greasing
1 16-ounce bag of frozen berries of your choice, or 2 cups of fresh
1 cup oats
1 teaspoon cinnamon
1/4 to 1/2 cup sugar, as desired
dash of salt

INSTRUCTIONS
1. Grease a 9 x 9 pan.
2. Dump the berries into the pan.
3. In a medium bowl, mix remaining ingredients and sprinkle on top of berries.
4. Bake at 350 degrees for 25 minutes. Let cool and enjoy.

Favorite Easy Family Dinner
SAUSAGE, PEPPER, AND POTATO SHEET-PAN DINNER

This is one of my family's favorite weekday meals. Even though it is so simple, everyone seems to love it. Best part? One pan!

INGREDIENTS
1 12-ounce package of chicken sausage, sliced
2 to 3 white potatoes, cubed
2 to 3 sweet potatoes, cubed
1 red bell pepper, cubed
1 green bell pepper, cubed
1 onion, cubed
olive oil

INSTRUCTIONS
1. Dump all your cut ingredients on a sheet pan, drizzle generously with olive oil, and sprinkle with salt and pepper.
2. Bake at 425 degrees for about 45 minutes; about halfway through, flip the food over.
3. Serve with ketchup, mustard, or hot sauce, if desired.

Favorite Thanksgiving Side Dish
MASHED POTATO STUFFING

This recipe came from Grammy's Lithuanian neighbor in Ringtown, Pennsylvania, and my aunt began making it for our Thanksgiving years ago. Once you try this recipe, I bet you will want it every Thanksgiving too. I have successfully made this recipe dairy and gluten free by substituting with dairy-free butter, unflavored coconut milk or almond milk, and a gluten-free sandwich bread.

INGREDIENTS
5 to 7 pounds white potatoes, washed and peeled
approximately 1 cup of milk (you need enough to make a soupy
   consistency)
1/4 cup butter
salt and pepper to taste
2/3 cup dried bread cubes
2 cups white onions, diced

1 cup celery, diced
1 stick of butter (½ cup)
2 tablespoons fresh parsley, roughly chopped

INSTRUCTIONS
1. Boil potatoes until soft. Then mash with enough milk, butter, salt, and pepper to make a soupy consistency, around 1 cup of liquid. They should be more watery than typical mashed potatoes.
2. Add ⅔ cup of dry bread cubes to potato mixture.
3. Sauté the onions and celery with 1 stick of butter. Add parsley.
4. Mix onion mixture with mashed potatoes.
5. Pour into a greased 9 x 13 pan. If you're making this at Thanksgiving, pour a bit of the juices from your roast turkey on top of the casserole.
6. Bake at 350 degrees until brown, about 30 to 45 minutes.

Favorite Comfort Food
MOM'S CHICKEN SOUP (WITH AUNT SARAH'S BUTTER ROLLS)

This meal will fix what ails ya! It is a labor of love but so worth it. Both recipes make a ton and freeze well.

BROTH INGREDIENTS
2 large white onions, chopped
5 celery stalks with leaves, chopped
5 to 6 cloves of garlic, chopped
1 cup carrots, chopped
1 whole organic chicken, washed
2 teaspoons kosher salt
1 teaspoon cracked black pepper
4 to 6 cups organic chicken stock, store bought or homemade
6 to 8 cups water (or enough to cover your chicken in the pot)

INSTRUCTIONS

1. Place all the ingredients in a very large stockpot. Cover and simmer for 1 to 3 hours.
2. Once the chicken has been simmering for several hours and is completely cooked, strain the chicken and vegetables, saving the broth. Pick meat off the chicken bones.
3. Save broth and chicken meat for soup.

SOUP INGREDIENTS

chicken broth (see recipe above) and reserved meat

1 to 2 cups fresh greens (spinach, kale, or parsley—or some combination of the three—are our favorites! Mom says to chop the greens *very* fine, as you would herbs, so that no one even knows they're in there!)

3 to 4 cups white potatoes

1 cup carrots, chopped

2 cups freshly cut corn

2 cups frozen peas

$\frac{1}{2}$ cup brown rice or barley (if desired)

1 cup of your choice: frozen dumplings or dried noodles (such as egg or orzo), if desired, rice (brown or white), or barley

INSTRUCTIONS

1. Bring broth to a boil.
2. Add greens (reserving a small handful), potatoes, and carrots. Return to a boil, and add chicken, corn, peas, and rice if you're using it.
3. Return to a boil again, and add frozen dumplings or noodles, if desired.
4. Once rice, dumplings, noodles and/or barley are cooked, add reserved fresh greens to the top of the pot, turn off the heat, and wait about ten minutes before serving.

AUNT SARAH'S BUTTER ROLLS

I'm not saying these are healthy. But, boy, are they good! We typically enjoy these only on Thanksgiving, Christmas, or Easter because . . . two sticks of butter!

INGREDIENTS
2 cups warm water
2 packets dry yeast
6 to 8 cups flour
2 sticks of butter, divided, plus more for brushing tops of rolls
1 tablespoon salt
1/2 cup sugar
1 egg

INSTRUCTIONS
1. Sprinkle yeast into warm water and let proof.
2. Put 2 cups of flour into a large mixing bowl. Add yeast and blend.
3. Melt 1 stick butter, salt, and sugar in a small pan, being careful not to burn. Add to flour mixture and blend.
4. Add 1 egg and mix well.
5. Add 4 to 6 cups of flour slowly. You want dough that sticks together in a ball without sticking to the sides of the bowl. Knead in a heavy-duty mixer or by hand for several minutes so you have an elastic dough.
6. Place dough in a large greased bowl, cover loosely, and let rise in a warm place until doubled in size. This will take at least an hour.
7. Dump dough onto floured surface, punch down, cover, and let rest for 10 minutes.
8. Knead dough until it has a solid, even texture and all lumps are gone. Roll out to half-inch thickness, then cut out rolls using biscuit cutter (you should have about 36).
9. Melt a stick of butter in an 11 x 15 or 10 x 13 pan. Dip rolls into the melted butter, fold in half, and pinch closed with your

fingers, then lay in the pan. Cover and let rise in warm place until doubled, about an hour.

10. Bake at 350 degrees for 20 minutes until golden brown. Remove from oven and brush with melted butter.

Yield: 3 dozen rolls

Favorite Thing to Serve a Bunch of Kids
SLUSHIES

This is so simple I hesitated to include it, but it has become such a tradition among the neighborhood kids that I have to share. It's especially great for summer afternoons when kids are sweaty, thirsty, and need a refreshing treat.

INGREDIENTS
1 64-ounce carton of juice or lemonade (our favorites: Aldi's organic lemonade or Trader Joe's peach juice or mango juice)
small plastic cups
small plastic spoons
crushed ice

INSTRUCTIONS
1. Fill cups 3/4 full with crushed ice.
2. Pour juice over and add spoon.
3. Serve to sweaty kids playing in your front yard and become a hero. (I warned you: it's really simple!)

CHAPTER 6

HOLIDAYS

Crooked Christmas Trees and Lingering Over Lent

Memory is the mother of traditions.

—NOËL PIPER[1]

THE HOLIDAYS ARE JUST THE BEST, AREN'T THEY? NO doubt they are some of the memories you treasure most. One year, Todd and I wanted to do something to make Christmas extra magical for our kids. We would get the Mother of All Christmas Trees. My dad had offered to sponsor our Christmas tree that year, so we thought, *What the heck? Let's get a mammoth tree. Our ceiling is high. Our kids are little. Let's go crazy.* 'Cause we're like that—crazy. (No, we're not.)

Everything went fine until Todd was in the garage a suspiciously long time "putting the tree in the stand." When I walked out to the garage, there was sawdust everywhere, a chainsaw running, and the stump whittled sharp like a pencil point but still ginormous. I had never once considered the importance of a good Christmas tree stand, and how your tree should fit in it. *Whoops.* Over the next three days the following events transpired:

- We decided we had no money to buy a new tree stand.
- Todd did something inventive with a piece of PVC pipe to fix our old tree stand.
- The tree fit but was crooked. And in an inconvenient new development, it fell over if you touched it.
- Todd went in the garage for two hours to do Smart Man Stuff to try to fix the situation.
- It was less crooked but swayed back and forth when you wiggled its branches. After a brief discussion, we decided an extremely unstable and mammoth tree is, in fact, a hazard for two toddler boys.
- Todd sawed the tree trunk down even more, and it stayed up until Aunt Jamee remarked how beautiful it was. It fell over before our eyes.
- Todd bought hooks, screws, string, and black camping rope to secure the tree to our window treatments. It looked like something out of a Pottery Barn catalog, more or less.
- While we decorated, Todd and I had a little *discussion* about whether icicle lights belong on a tree (they don't, ever) while the boys broke a vintage ornament, played tug of war with Christmas lights, and dumped out all twenty-five verses of the Advent calendar.
- I asked Todd what we should do next about our crooked, redneck, wobbly Christmas tree and the mess all over the place. "Cry," he said.
- Eight fittings, three sawings, two hooks, and one PVC pipe later, Todd went to Lowe's to get a new Christmas tree stand. Which we clearly should have done in the first place.

Nothing is ever perfect when you're trying to make memories. Mine is a funny example, but many times it's not funny at all. Many times the wounds are deep. If you have a broken family, holidays may be more stressful and sad than special. If you've lost someone, times of celebration can be painful and grief-ridden instead. Maybe you exert much work to make special memories, and no one seems to appreciate it. *What do we do with holiday heartbreak?*

I love the holidays, and I have so many tips and traditions for you to consider. But I have an inkling what you need more than ideas *is the reminder that it's worth it.* It's worth celebrating when you feel like your family or your life is a colossal, crooked, and falling-over mess.

SPECIAL CELEBRATIONS ARE WORTH IT

Yes, I believe it is *always* worth it to celebrate all our treasured holidays even though they will rarely feel perfect. When we celebrate, we remind ourselves what matters in this life. "Celebrations are the ritualized interruptions in the continuum of daily life which remind us who we are, where we came from and where we are going."[2]

When I was a child, Good Friday and Easter celebrations were anchors in my family life, with a deep, visceral reminder every year that Jesus died and Jesus rose. Not one single Easter went by without a pausing, a noting, a celebrating. We always attended a Good Friday service with my grandparents. Every year, at the end of the service, the lights dimmed, and my uncle stepped out of his pew and walked to the front, holding his hammer and three nails. I can hear it like it was two minutes ago. Pound, pound, pound, pound. Totally dark church. In went the nails to a piece of wood. The spooky solemnity conjured up powerful feelings of repentance in the younger me. Thirty years later I can still hear it, can still feel my heartbeat rising. As a child, I knew I was a sinner. I could feel it—my deep shame and my gratitude that Someone endured something so awful, for me. He. Died. For. Me. (With each pounded nail.)

Christmas was the same. Over and over, the well-made melamine nativity, the knitted stockings from Aunt Jamee, the handed-down, thread-wrapped balls hanging on a real tree. These things were constants. They happened every year. They

> When we celebrate, we remind ourselves what matters in this life.

meant something. They tied us to something larger than ourselves. They happened and continued to happen whether Dad was traveling or had lost his job, whether Mom was sick, whether we were moving, whether *anything*. They were constants and taught me what mattered.

Since the holidays are an integral part of our culture, these special days form the core of our family's treasured memories. We are in prime memory-making territory here, mamas. Whether it's Christmas and Easter or Thanksgiving and Mother's Day, I believe that when these special days come, we have the perfect chance to celebrate what we value in a whimsical, memorable way. Even when it's hard, even when nothing seems to go right, we keep at it, we repeat the traditions yearly, and the family knows, remembers, learns again: this is valuable to us.

GOOD, BETTER, AND BEST CELEBRATIONS

It's worth it to celebrate, but does it matter *how* we celebrate? Are all holiday traditions created equally? If you search "Christmas activities," for example—oh, my goodness! So many options! How does one even choose? I don't recommend this search, by the way, if you're prone to heart palpitations and sudden increases of blood pressure. Here are just a few of the many options available to the average mother these days: you could hide an elf, hide a star, bake a birthday cake, prep shoeboxes, exchange gifts, exchange ornaments, read no shortage of excellent seasonally appropriate books morning, afternoon, and night.

You could celebrate twelve days of Christmas, have a shepherd's feast, go caroling in your neighborhood, sing to the elderly, serve at a soup kitchen, make cookies for firemen, pastors, or neighbors. You could read the Old Testament prophecies, memorize the names of Jesus or the Christmas passage in Luke. You could craft reindeer, Santas, or bells out of popsicle sticks and pom-poms. You could paint wooden manger scenes and create Christmas trees out of handprints.

Are you overwhelmed yet? As I type these words, there are thirty-one days until Christmas and I'm breaking an anxious sweat, so I think I'll stop. Never in the history of Christmases has a culture been so inundated with ways to celebrate as we are today.

Then a handful of citizens have just had enough, so there's the countermovement. The easy-button holiday. These are the kind souls who sense our weepy overwhelm and snuggle up beside us. "It's okay. Christmas doesn't have to be anything special. You can eat take-out Chinese food on paper plates and exchange unwrapped gift cards, and no one will be the wiser."

So which one is it? Are we doomed to Decembers chock-full of Pinterest crafts and whirlwind festivities? Are we bad moms if we never make shamrock-shaped pancakes or never have perfectly coordinated Easter outfits? Or are we totally off the hook, and we can just wing it each holiday? *How do we know what's the best use of our time?*

I believe that there is a *good* and a *better*. With our limited time, we must be strategic in celebrating. There are so many super-fun traditions for holidays, and I'm going to share lots of these ideas. *Yet the traditions and rituals that strengthen our faith and our families are the ones that deserve the bulk of our time and energy.*

To Make It Count, Plan Ahead

Planning ahead is huge. This is a lesson I have learned slowly. The first few years I was a mom, I would see Cadbury eggs at the pharmacy check-out counter in mid-March and realize, "Oh, my goodness. Easter is in ten days." (These were the sleep-deprived years where I would do things like get in the shower with my socks on and put my car keys in the freezer, so please don't be too hard on me.) I realized it is hard to appreciate fully the depth of a holiday when you have ten days to unpack it with a child. So I have learned to plan ahead for our celebrations.

See, parenting through holidays not only requires in-the-moment work (such as the apple-peeling, present-wrapping, cookie-frosting, bread-kneading types of labor) but also the labor of preparing. This has been especially true for me at Christmas and Easter. It took me thirty-six years to realize how much these holidays have in common; *namely, that there is an element of waiting.* Easter has Lent; Christmas has Advent. We anticipate Christ's birth in Advent, and with heavy responsibility ponder His death and resurrection in Lent.[3] We are waiting in both. Your family can't do much "thoughtful waiting" if it is suddenly Holy Week and you haven't mentioned once that Jesus died on the cross.

What this means on a practical level is that once Halloween is over, I am thinking of our Advent activities. Easter presents its own challenges, with the changing date every year. But even while it's cold and barren in January, I'm noting Ash Wednesday and marking down when I should begin pulling out the Easter books. When these special waiting seasons of Lent and Advent start, I am ready.

I have our waiting tools on hand, whether that is a Jesse tree or an Advent calendar in Christmas or a Lenten activity in the spring.

You may be thinking, *This sounds like an incredible amount of work and planning.* Yes, exactly. What I am challenging us to do is to prioritize our spiritual celebrations.

Make changes to your daily family life during December and mid-March. Advent and Lent matter more and should take precedence over normal routines. Sit down and pray about the upcoming holiday. Put some things on hold. Take some of your precious time and strategize. Ask yourself, *Right now, in my family, with the kids the ages they are, how can we honor these holidays?* What needs to go? To pause? To be set aside temporarily to focus on Jesus? What activities would help us as a family choose the eternal over the won't-really-matter-in-the-long-run?

I know what I am saying is crazy sauce in today's culture. Who would say no to a birthday party because you opt to sit in candlelight and read about the crucifixion instead? Who would say, "I'm sorry; I can't do that fun thing, because I actually need to stay home today and plan our Advent activities"? It's crazy, weird, and costly. It takes work, and it takes planning. *But it is worth it.* We are meeting our goals of seeing our kids connected to our faith, bonded to lasting traditions, and impressed with the eternal. It is a sacrifice worth making.

When All This Seems Like Too Much

These are all wonderful thoughts, but have you ever been in a season where you just didn't feel like celebrating? One year I had not one but two miscarriages within eight weeks. By the time the second happened, it was nearly Easter. If I had read this chapter during those days, I would have sobbed. I couldn't plan or celebrate anything that year. Gratefully, I had a friend who dropped off Easter outfits for my boys (what an act of kindness!), another made me a set of Resurrection Eggs, and several more brought meals. I didn't do anything to make Easter memories that year. But, then again, I received grace, I prayed, and I needed God a lot. That, too, was a type of commemorating who God is and what He continues to do in my life.

There are those seasons, and if you arrive in one, may you feel the Father's love, and may it fill the empty spaces in your heart.

THE GIFT OF CHRISTMAS

Whether you're slogging through the holidays dutifully or can't wait for them to arrive, here are some practical ideas for celebrating Christmas as a family. I talked earlier about the good and better ways to celebrate; I'd say these Advent rituals are well worth your time and effort.

Daily Rituals During Advent
- We always have an Advent calendar or two running. The *Star from Afar* book is wonderful for toddlers and preschoolers, as you hide a star and read a short verse about Jesus each day. Ann Voskamp's *Unwrapping the Greatest Gift: A Family Celebration of Christmas* is a darling family Advent calendar with winsome devotions that I think are ideal for elementary-aged children or older.
- Another low-budget Advent option is to use an Advent calendar you already have and each day read a Bible story leading up to Jesus' birth. For example, we love *The Jesus Storybook Bible*. Find the story about Jesus' birth in this Bible, and then flip back twenty-five stories. Start there on December 1, and on December 25, you'll be at the story of Jesus' birth.
- Another idea is to wrap up all your Christmas-themed picture

books, then unwrap and read one each day in Advent. Our collection includes a few nonmeaningful stories about mittens and snow, but we keep adding more of our favorite Gospel-centered Christmas books each year. Two of our very favorites are *One Wintry Night* by Ruth Graham (a chapter book that is ideal for elementary-aged kids) and the picture book *The Crippled Lamb* by Max Lucado. Another Advent activity is to light candles daily, adding one each week until Christmas. We incorporated this into our homeschool time and the kids loved it.

- If you have teenagers, read through an Advent devotional together. For parents and teens, I highly recommend *Unwrapping the Names of Jesus* by Asheritah Ciuciu and *The Greatest Gift* by Ann Voskamp.

Christmas Bucket List

Each year our family makes a Christmas bucket list for the miscellaneous things we want to do during the holiday. A bucket list is a good way to let traditions grow with you. I write out the days in December, and we fill it with different activities—whatever we choose that year. My kids are still in the younger years, so our staples include making cookies to take to Dad at work, neighborhood caroling, inviting a single person we know over for dinner, and driving to see Christmas lights. A service-centered twist: pick an act of kindness for each day in Advent.

Balancing Holiday Fun with Christ-Centered Meaning

I'll be the first one to tell you that I am simply overwhelmed sometimes with balancing the whole thing of Christmas. There is fun seasonal stuff, like reindeer crafts, ice skating, and cookie decorating, that I don't want to throw out entirely. But I know the reason for the season is our Savior Jesus. Some families use the calendar itself as a way to structure their celebrations. They celebrate the whimsy of gifts and wintry fun during certain times of the month and focus on Christ specifically for other parts of the month.

Consider the Frank family, for example. Because December 6 is Saint Nicholas Day—honoring the amazing man who became famous for his gift-giving—they open their stockings on this day. Then the focus transitions to Jesus for the remainder of the season. On Christmas morning they receive a few small gifts from Mom and Dad, but that's not the primary focus of the day. Then on January 6, the day of Epiphany, celebrating the wise men's gifts, the kids give their gifts to each other and maybe receive one joint gift from their parents.[4] I like this way of designating certain times for celebrating one another, which still allows plenty of time to focus fully on Christ's birth.

Another Christ-honoring Christmas tradition is to give a gift to Jesus. Throughout the Christmas season, kids do jobs to earn money and maybe also offer some of their previously saved money. Maybe the parents set aside some of their Christmas budget for Jesus' gift as well. On Christmas Eve the family places their money inside their stockings, and the money is given to someone in need. (It might seem odd to little ones that we give Jesus' gift to someone else, but let's remind them that it's biblical. In His own words, Jesus says that whatever we do for the least of these, we have done for Him.[5]) Then on Christmas morning in everyone's stocking is a small gift in place of the money, reinforcing the concept that God cares for those who give to Him in faith.[6] I love this way of gift-giving. Simple, warm, and connected to Jesus' birthday.

Thoughts on Gift-Giving

There is a wide range of what Christian families consider to be good and healthy in terms of Christmas gifts. Many families do one small gift; some give no gifts. I was intrigued by Edith Schaeffer's suggestion that if you don't do gifts for each other during Christmas, you should make sure you bless each other with gifts another day in the year.[7]

I think it's wise to set limits for your family gifts so you don't fall into the trap that anything less than a colossal *mountain* of plastic knickknacks and electronic gadgets under the tree is weird, abnormal, and insufficient. Your Christmas morning gift-giving should be reasonable. Our family has simplified our gift-giving to four gifts: something you want, something you need, something you wear, something you read.

Even with this simplification, there still seem to be oodles of gifts for teachers, family, and friends to find and wrap. My friend Page blessed me infinitely with her shopping tip: "I do all my shopping before December 1, so we can focus on Jesus for the month."[8] I have followed her advice ever since. Mid-November, I make my list and boom, boom, knock the items off. I realized that my previous habit of dragging my feet with shopping didn't ensure that my presents were more thoughtful. I can be just as creative and intentional with my earlier deadline.

So, gifts out of the way, in December we focus on our Christmas bucket list and daily Advent activities. We focus on outreach. We wait. Sometimes with giddy, childish anticipation. Sometimes with quiet longings for Jesus to be all that He is, to be the King of our broken world.

Cleaning for Jesus

Also, we clean. I had not linked holy Advent-waiting with cleaning until I read the most wonderful little Christmas story called *The Light at Tern Rock* by Julia L. Sauer. A boy and his aunt are stuck in a lonely lighthouse for Christmas. It's a disappointing fate, yet they ready the place with joy. They scrub, they dust, they wash and wipe, they light all the candles and drag in greenery, they don the table with a feast comprising everything delicious they have. Their humble dwelling is clean, beautiful, and ready. And in the process, so become their hearts.

Admittedly, I have a soft spot in my heart for a well-scrubbed floor (a longing yet to be satisfied since entering motherhood). For this reason, their little Advent cleaning ceremony touched me deeply. I tried it one year. I told the kids: before we get the Christmas stuff out, we're going to get this house ready for Jesus. Beautiful and clean for Jesus. I know in my heart that Jesus would come to a house where the toilet had grime around the ring, yet I can't deny it: this ritual was undeniably powerful. We did our best, dusting and scrubbing windows till they shone. We were all so pleased when the house was clean. We'd done it for Jesus.

THE GIFT OF EASTER

As I was reading in Noël Piper's *Treasuring God in Our Traditions*, I was convicted of how I've viewed Easter. Noël says, "We reveal to ourselves and others what is important to us by the way that we celebrate."[9] Are we focusing, she wonders, on the special outfits, the Easter baskets, the groceries and meal prep, the packing lists for all the trips we'll go on? Or are we setting aside time to ponder and focus on what Christ's death and resurrection mean?[10]

As Christians, Easter should be precious to us. The time we spend remembering and honoring Christ's loving sacrifice is time well spent. So a few weeks before Lent begins, I pray. I ask for wisdom, that God would show me how this season can be a special reminding-time for my kids. As you do the same, here are a few suggestions.

Easter Ideas for Young Children

- With Resurrection Eggs, you open one egg each day during the twelve days before Easter, similar to an Advent calendar. Each contains an item of meaning to the Easter story. The book *Benjamin's Box* by Melody Carlson is a fictional account created to read each day along with the egg opening. You can purchase Resurrection Eggs or find instructions on how to make your own.
- Read *The Jesus Storybook Bible*, or another children's Bible, in the days leading up to the resurrection. I simply count back fourteen stories from the resurrection story to see where I should start. I have read that it's best to begin celebrating with little ones about two weeks prior to Easter. That's enough time to discuss, but not so far ahead that they lose focus.
- Tell the story of the Holy Week with LEGOs, Play-Doh, or other small items around the house.
- Decorate an Easter tree with items that are meaningful to Jesus' life and death. This idea is fully explained in Noël Piper's book *Treasuring God in Our Traditions*.
- Bake hot cross buns or Resurrection Rolls on Easter morning. Resurrection Rolls are fun because after baking, there's an empty hole inside just like the empty grave.

Easter Ideas for Elementary-Aged Children

- Read biblical fiction based on the Easter story. Two of our favorites are *Jotham's Journey* and *Amon's Adventure* by Arnold Ytreeide. These are well-written, gripping historical fiction tales that bring the Easter story to life. (Be advised that these stories are intense at parts, so use discretion when reading to young children.)
- Build a resurrection garden. You can get inspiration in numerous places online. You create a beautiful miniature garden

with a representation of the hill of Golgotha and the empty
tomb.

- Recreate the Passover Seder meal and Jesus' washing of the
disciples' feet. This Jewish celebration is a meaning-packed,
reverent meal that brings the Last Supper to life.
- Help your kids build and paint a wooden cross to keep or
give as a gift. They could add a phrase ("Jesus died for me,"
"Jesus Lives," and so on).

Easter Ideas for Older Children

- Participate in a family media fast during Holy Week or all
of Lent. (Note: I recommend not to mandate giving things
up for Lent but to offer the suggestion, to set the example,
and to encourage and champion your kids if they decide to
join you.)
- Watch a movie about Easter together as a family. I'd recommend *The Greatest Story Ever Told*, *The Passion of the Christ*,
or *The Jesus Movie*. (Some of these are rather intense, so use
discretion with younger children.)
- Consider downloading a devotional app for Lent to go through
with the family.
- Prioritize attending a Good Friday service as a family.

Lent Should Be Solemn

Despite the cheery decorations, lovingly filled baskets, and
coordinating outfits I love about the season, there is a definite
heaviness surrounding Easter that's supposed to be there. We honor
this by allowing ourselves to live in this sadness and waiting. This
requires some time, as moms, to retreat from the daily press of our
responsibilities, to listen, to quiet our souls and ponder.

If you haven't been consistent with daily Bible reading and
prayer, Lent is an ideal time to begin. I've also found that it's very

rewarding to attend church services during Holy Week. Usually there are a million other things I'd prefer to do at the time, but I always end up feeling so grateful for the rich reminder that comes by singing Easter hymns and hearing the story of Holy Week read aloud with other believers. These sorts of events are usually very conducive to visitors, so if you don't attend a church with a Maundy Thursday or Good Friday service, then visit one near you that does have the service.

THE GIFT OF THANKSGIVING

My extended family gathers almost every year for a Thanksgiving meal of epic proportions. The masterpiece of my mom and Aunt Marci, this meal is a true work of art. It has been my favorite holiday since I was a child. (If you want to know why, be sure to try the recipe for Mashed Potato Stuffing in chapter 5.)

Now that there's a whole slew of kids in the mix, we've added some different traditions besides simply passing out on the couch after extended helpings of macaroni and cheese. After the meal has been eaten, we gather around my parents' outdoor fireplace to sing praise songs with the guitar. The kids each take turns saying something they're thankful for, from A to Z. This is a simple activity, but it begins the habit of practicing regular gratefulness to God for His gifts. Here are a few simple traditions to consider for your Thanksgiving celebrations.

Thanksgiving Ideas for Young Children
- Enjoy reading or listening to stories about the first Thanksgiving.
- Organize a Thanksgiving craft for the kids.
- Join a Turkey Trot race or have your own by jogging through the neighborhood.

- Let the kids decorate the Thanksgiving tables with acorns, pinecones, and colorful leaves from the yard.

Thanksgiving Ideas for Older Children

- Play a family football game in the backyard.
- Serve dinner at a soup kitchen.
- Have them design family T-shirts if you're having a big re-union on the holiday.
- Let them make a unique dish to contribute to the meal.
- They can choose a psalm to read before the Thanksgiving meal.

OTHER HOLIDAY CELEBRATIONS

There are nearly as many holidays as there are families who cele-brate them. Here some fun ideas for you to consider as you celebrate other holidays together:

Valentine's Day

- Make cookies with gobs of icing and deliver to Dad at his office.
- Look for stickers, doilies, hearts, stamps, and ribbons on sale all year long and save them up. Then, drag it all out and make a Valentine's Day *mess* while making cards for everyone you know and love.
- Give your daughters flowers. My dad always did this, and especially when we were older it sure was nice to get flowers on a particularly lonely Valentine's Day (even if it *was* from dear old Dad).
- Consider having a fancy dinner with your whole family on Valentine's Day, and then go out another less-crowded night that week with your husband.

- Make your little ones a handmade valentine, even a simple construction-paper heart. I am always shocked at how pleased my kids are with a valentine from Mom.

New Year's Eve (and New Year's Day)
- Make a list of your family's answered prayers from the past year.
- Share the highs and lows of your year and reflect on what God has taught you.
- Have a game night, movie marathon, or dance party with the kids on New Year's Eve. For older children, you could organize a cooking challenge or contest for the meal. For example, everyone could make an appetizer and have judges vote on a favorite.
- Cook Beans and Greens on New Year's Day. This Southern tradition mixes black-eyed peas with greens, such as collards, mustard, or turnip. Serve it with corn bread.
- Begin a Bible reading plan together.

Saint Patrick's Day
- Saint Patrick was an amazing man, so pick up a good storybook and read with your kids about his life. I recommend *The Story of St. Patrick: More Than Shamrocks and Leprechauns* by Voice of the Martyrs.
- Cook an Irish meal, especially if your family has Irish blood. A few ideas are corned beef and cabbage, beef stew, or shepherd's pie served with Irish soda bread.

Mother's Day
- Serve Mom breakfast in bed, or let the kids help cook a Mother's Day brunch.
- My family has a sweet tradition that my husband and sons always fill up my flower pots on Mother's Day. Every year,

they ring the doorbell, sprint out of sight, and then wait for my reaction when I see the new plants.

- Look outward and consider if there are women who would be blessed by a visit, flowers, or a phone call. Maybe you know women who have experienced loss, who long to be wives or mothers but are not, or whose children live out of state. Who could your family bless with a simple reminder that she is loved on this often-emotional day?

- If you are an adoptive mom, Mother's Day may bring a host of complicated emotions. If your child feels the desire to honor his or her birth mother, perhaps you could do so by lighting a candle or planting a flower in her honor.

Father's Day

- Take an annual camping or hiking trip over Father's Day weekend.

- Have the kids fill out a fun questionnaire about Dad or Grandpa to give to him. (These are always a hoot in our family!)

- Go fishing.

- Ask Dad, "What do *you* want to do today?" Sometimes we moms have our own ideas of how Father's Day should go, but we may be surprised at what our husbands say would be life-giving to them.

Independence Day

- Do some patriotic crafts. (In my family we each paint a flag picture, and then we solicit votes on social media for the favorite.)

- Make a patriotic food, such as patriotic pancakes with berries and whipped cream or a cake decorated like a flag.

- Listen to our national anthem.

- Gather with the neighbors to enjoy sparklers and small fireworks in the street.

Juneteenth

This American holiday commemorates the abolition of slavery on June 19, 1865, when the last slaves were freed in Texas. This is a significant holiday, particularly in black culture, and worth observing by all Americans as we honor the day that gave freedom to all. You may be able to attend a local Juneteenth celebration in your community, or you can also honor this day by reading a biography of black pioneers in American history.

Halloween

Growing up, I didn't really celebrate Halloween. After I had my own little ones, we had some rather awkward discussions when my toddlers noticed interesting Halloween decorations in our neighbors' yards, like skeletons clawing their way out of pretend graves or ghosts with nooses around their necks. Yikes! However, we have found some ways to redeem this often-creepy holiday through engaging with our neighbors. Through our hospitality, inevitably we will meet a neighbor we have never met before. While it's still not my favorite, this holiday has become one of our neighborhood's treasured traditions. Here are some fun, non-creepy Halloween traditions to consider:

- Host a giant block party, complete with a box maze for the kids and a chili cook-off for the adults.
- Provide homemade cider for parents who are walking with their kids by your house.
- Have a children's costume parade down your street before dark.
- And of course, October 31 is also Reformation Day, so you

can honor Martin Luther by reading a biography on him, by singing "A Mighty Fortress Is Our God," or, on a goofy note, by eating gummy worms to teach about the Diet of Worms (the name of Luther's trial).

There are just so, so many ways to celebrate, aren't there? I hope you're armed with ideas and encouragement to pick a few of these ideas to bless your family. Don't get discouraged if the going gets tough (or the Christmas trees start falling over). Celebrations are basically a pressure cooker where all of parenting—the wonder, whimsy, sweat, annoyances, let-downs, dish washings, clothes ironings, and squirmy story readings—are swirled into one glorious memory. It's a lot of work, and that is okay. It is the good work.

THINGS TO CONSIDER

As you brainstorm your own family traditions, here are some things to consider:

- What are some favorite holiday traditions from your childhood?
- How stressed do you usually feel during the Christmas or Easter season? Is it the good kind of stress of celebrating well, or are there things you could eliminate from your holiday busyness?
- Can you think of ways to honor the waiting and the heaviness of Easter?
- Do you (or did you growing up) have a Thanksgiving tradition that encouraged gratitude?
- What's your favorite minor holiday? Would you like to add other traditions to this day?

SUGGESTED THINGS TO DO

- Make a Christmas bucket list, including fun, service, and spiritual activities.
- Write down one Easter tradition you'd like to implement.
- Evaluate your Christmas gift-giving procedure. Is this something you'd like to tweak?
- Begin building a home library of meaningful books for Easter and Christmas. (See my blog's resource page for suggested books.[11])
- Create a holiday calendar that helps you plan each year in advance. Set alerts on your phone when it's time to begin planning each one.

CHAPTER 7

LEARNING

Cultivating Curiosity

What we learn with pleasure, we never forget.
—ALFRED MERCIER[1]

TEN YEARS AGO, WHILE VERY PREGNANT, I COZIED myself into our living room chair and plopped my feet up on the ottoman. I had just arrived at that blessed point in pregnancy where one can begin to use one's stomach as a sort of perch for things. Stuffed into one side of the chair was a box of jalapeño-flavored Cheez-Its, on which I absolutely overdosed during my first and second pregnancies. (Needless to say, I will never see them in quite the same way again. If I try real hard, I can sort of taste them now, and it's not pleasant.) Using my right hand to scoop and re-scoop handfuls of Cheez-Its, I had my left hand free to turn the pages of the book sitting on my tummy. You couldn't have told it from the utter commonness of the moment, what with the Cheez-It crumbs in my stomach folds and whatnot, but my life was about to be changed.

I was reading this ugly little booklet that simply could not be more unassuming. The cover read, *Echo in Celebration: A Call to Home-Centered Education.*[2] I have no idea what would have possessed me to pick up this small book on one of my last remaining evenings as a childless adult. I can only chalk it up to divine Providence.

I read the first chapter with my heart beating wildly. The author, Leigh Bortins, describes their life as a homeschooling family climbing Mount Saint Helens, swimming in the Mississippi River, hiking the Rockies, building a sand beach for their lake house, eating a picnic dinner in the dark under a full moon, and fishing for turtles.

I brushed the crumbs off my stomach and reread the first chapter in its entirety to my husband, who was not *quite* as overcome with emotion as I was (par for the course), but he did agree to future discussions about our children's education. Though he did wonder, *Could we perhaps wait until, say, the first one leaves the womb to make any permanent decisions about schooling?* What can you even do with someone so exasperatingly rational?

I couldn't help it. This book had done something to me. I had been in schools all my life, first as a student, then as an educator. But somewhere in that first chapter, something clicked within me as I resolved, *I want my kids to learn like that.*

Before you're tempted to suspect me of a covert operation to convert everyone to homeschooling, rest assured, I have no such plans. The kind of home I am describing can absolutely happen whether you homeschool or not. I've seen it done very well in homes where kids attend conventional school. Whatever your schooling choice, taking kids on learning adventures can make some of your best memories. Some may be once-in-a-lifetime experiences your family will treasure, and others may become beloved traditions you look forward to repeating year after year.

LEARNING CAN BE FUN

"Learning adventures" may not sound like a barrel of laughs to you. Typically when we hear the word *learning*, we think *school*, and long nights at the kitchen table extracting division out of a fourth grader may not be anyone's most treasured family memory. No, when we're talking about learning adventures, you can dismiss workbooks, SAT-prep courses, or boring biology textbooks. We are forging new territory. We are learning adventurers, intellectual discoverers. We are going to experience the joy of learning together!

Can you tell I'm simply bursting at the seams with ideas to spark curiosity in your home? I am. But this first: Do you remember my letter to memory-making moms in the beginning of the book? Do you remember my encouragement that you can't do it all? Yes, that again. Take a deep breath with me.

At this point we're seven chapters into the book, and I've shot at you about 2,456 tradition ideas, like balls from an automatic tennis ball machine. You may be feeling a little overwhelmed at this juncture. Maybe even discouraged.

I have felt that too. I have read those books that list all the *amazing things* you could do. I've read them, and I feel awful afterward. I'll think, *Well, that's nice for you, Mrs. Author, that your life is so perfect!* Mama reading this, don't you let that despair creep in this time. Just put away all the "It's too lates" and "I'll nevers." Remember the saying, *I can't do it all, but we can make some beautiful memories?* With this reminder to take what we can and leave the rest, let's jump in.

THE GIFT OF LEARNING WITH TODDLERS

When I began doing preschool with my little babies at home—because, you know, former teacher, chomping at the bit to get started—I honestly thought that all good learning involved some sort of photocopied worksheet. My poor boys were three and one years old. (I know!) They'd just recently begun forming sentences together, yet (I cringe to think it) I made them sit still at a table fumbling with a chubby pencil to complete their worksheets.

Thankfully, by some sort of fortunate alignment of the stars, I was gifted with a mother-in-law, Carole, who had taught kindergarten for twenty-four years. One day she showed up at my door with five large crates filled to the brim with stuff she called "manipulatives." They looked suspiciously like toys to me, but she kept pretending they were real learning devices, so I thought I would humor her for a little bit. She cuddled up to my three-year-old son with dress-up hats, colored beads, and craft pipe cleaners, saying things like, "You see, his work is play. That's what he needs to do."

> For a good long while in the home, learning is play and play is learning.

It was all quite disconcerting. I had file folders and envelopes chock-full of photocopied worksheets he needed to be working on, and there she was, distracting him with games, pattern blocks, tower building, and science experiments.

Boy, are my kids fortunate she stepped in!

Of course, Carole was right. Stimulating play and engaging conversation are the best places to start toward lifelong learning. For a good long while in the home, learning is play and play is learning.

THE GIFT OF READING TOGETHER

And of course, read lots of books! At some point in each of my children's early childhood, I would worry, "He doesn't like reading! She has no interest!" Then, lo and behold, as I faithfully read picture books aloud, not worrying if they climbed down or meandered away in the middle, each child eventually developed a love of books. And then there's the part where they love books *so much*. Too much. At every spare minute, they want you to read. I try to never say no when children ask me to read to them. If need be, I'll say, "In ten minutes," and my goal is to honor that.

Sarah Mackenzie's *The Read-Aloud Family* reminded me of the power of story in the home. "When we read about characters—both factual and fictional—experiencing hardship and meeting injustice, something moves within us. That something is empathy—the beginning of compassion. It is a tremendous gift we give to our children every time we crack the pages of a book."[3]

One ritual we relish is reading novels over lunch. (Bonus: it means less time to argue over whose limp cucumber is plopped in someone else's quadrant at the table.) We usually have a novel we're working through at bedtime too. My husband particularly enjoys reading Roald Dahl or C. S. Lewis novels to the kids at night. I love these evening reading times; they're experiencing literature together, and I get to take a homeschool mom time-out while Dad takes over.

It seems weird to think that you could make memories together when you never leave the couch. But we all know, of course, that a good book is its own sort of adventure. "If families don't read books together, how do they know each other's friends? Reading aloud as a family has bound us together, as sharing an adventure always does. We know the same people. We have gone through emotional crisis together."[4] Reading together bonds a family as few other experiences can do—and all for the cost of a library card (nothing!) and a few minutes on the couch.

THE GIFT OF FIELD TRIPS

Sometimes leaving your home for a good, old-fashioned field trip is just the thing you need. We live in a time absolutely saturated with learning opportunities. Make the most of them during your family time. We have the most amazing raptor sanctuary near us. I assumed birds would be one of the more boring animals for young boys, but was I ever wrong! We go to this raptor center routinely, and all my kids are fascinated by the owls, vultures, and falcons housed there. Create a family bucket list for learning opportunities. You might include a visit to a Smithsonian museum, a Civil War battleground, or important local monuments. Don't let silly things like living in remote parts of the country deter you. Where there's a will, there's a way.

I still remember the time my parents took us to Williamsburg, Virginia, to learn about Colonial American life. Unfortunately for my parents, they elected to designate this a "surprise" trip, where the destination was kept secret from us kids. In hindsight, Colonial Williamsburg may have been a bigger hit with us had we not been envisioning Disney World or Six Flags as our destination. Nevertheless, I still remember meandering through the cobblestone streets, eating authentic Colonial meals (it felt like Thanksgiving), and seeing fascinating characters fully dressed in the clothing of the time.

After New Year's Day, I take a Mom's planning day to choose goals and activities for our family for the coming year. I like to choose one educational site or experience per season to enjoy as a family. This year it's listening to Handel's *Messiah* at Christmas, visiting a historical site in the spring, a planetarium in the summer, and the zoo in the fall.

Here's the thing about family field trips: you win some, you lose some—like the "World Famous Tiger Adventure" we visited on a whim. Personally, I'm just grateful we all lived to tell about this day. Right away, we noticed that the tigers were a little too close for our liking. And by "too close for our liking," I mean we had a brief discussion about whether we should leave and call the police.

Basically, there were several feet of shredded chicken wire separating us from one of the world's fiercest beasts. The habitats were natural, that is, if tigers in their native habitat play with dilapidated playground equipment and eat rotten watermelons. Did I mention it was about 1,456 degrees outside that day? What were we thinking? The final straw: the feed for the tigers contained some of my son's allergens, which added an extra rush of adrenaline for Todd and me as we tried to steer clear of it. Ultimately I wish we had saved our $97 (or whatever it was) and just continued on down the road. But I mention this to point out that not every excursion will be an idyllic experience. Then again, we all have a memory to laugh over now.

INSTILLING CURIOSITY

The world is a fascinating place. It's just a matter of seeing learning opportunities everywhere. For example, I have always been a weather watcher. My family makes fun of me for my "tornado updates." (But, seriously, if I have to explain the difference between a "watch" and a "warning" one more time, I don't know what I will do with these people.) Now, my kids and I enjoy tracking storms and talking up weather patterns together. This is a prime example of an adage from my days as a teacher: *if you are excited, they will be excited.*

One winter our weatherman had been discussing an "arctic chill pattern" (an unusual pattern of frigid air) heading toward us.

My five-year-old asked, "Will we be having an Arctic Chill Party?" It just seemed obvious. We celebrate everything, so of course we'd celebrate this momentous event too. We make a big deal of the solar eclipse, the election, and the massive construction project happening outside our neighborhood. There are always things to look forward to, discuss, wonder about, and count down to.

Are there topics that interest you? Maybe you're not a weather girl like me, but you love architecture, yoga, cooking, birds, Shakespeare, constellations, or essential oils. Involve your children in what you love. They'll naturally feed off your enthusiasm. Even if they never re-create your crème brûlée or match your crocheting prowess, the shared memories of learning together can become a tradition of its own.

And guess what? It works both ways. What do your kids love that you may know nothing about? I'll never forget the time my eight-year-old crept out of bed, clutching a book to his chest. "Mom," he said with gravity, "you *have* to read this Hardy Boys book. Mom, you'll *love* it." This openness to learning what they love may require you to join in all kinds of unnatural things through the years, like play Mario Kart, catch a curve ball, try a Zumba class, or listen to music you normally wouldn't otherwise.

SCHOOL TRADITIONS

Whether you homeschool or your kids are enrolled in a private school or public school, here are a few ideas for some fun school-related traditions:

- Take the kids on a date with Mom or Dad the week before school starts.
- Host a Back-to-School Prayer Breakfast in your home on the

Saturday before school starts. Neighbors can come to enjoy pancakes and scrambled eggs and then pray for all the kids heading back to school. One family who hosted this said that even families who didn't regularly attend church grew to love this day to pray over the school year.[5]

- Have the "back-to-school fairy" leave special (school-related) treats under your kids' pillows.
- Start a messy and memorable first-day-of-school-smash-cake tradition. The day before school begins, each kid makes a giant cupcake with frosting and decorates it. When the kids come home from school after their first day, they dive face-first into the smash cake.[6]
- On the last day of school, greet the kids at the bus stop with a water gun ambush. Pack sandwiches and juice boxes and head straight to the neighborhood pool to celebrate summer.
- Celebrate the last day of school by tent camping in the backyard.

TECHNOLOGY AS SERVANT, NOT MASTER

I've learned to appreciate the value of treating media events as special occasions. Instead of cultivating the daily habit of "popping on a show" or handing someone an iPad, I try instead to choose ahead of time the technology I really love and then savor it as a family. Don't get me wrong; I've survived a few rough seasons of motherhood thanks to regular showings of *Thomas the Train*, and there just are those times—potty training while nursing a newborn comes to mind, in particular. But when I regain the bandwidth, we recalibrate. We proactively select really great shows, movies, or apps, and we choose the right times to enjoy them.

Media was impactful in my own life as a child, from the amazing *Adventures in Odyssey* audio tapes we listened to every road trip, to the heartwarming shows I loved as a girl, such as *Lassie* and *Old Yeller*. I remember the time I watched *It's a Wonderful Life* in a season of preadolescent angst, and it brought such light and comfort to me.

Goodness, I'm a blogger! I certainly understand the doors that technology can open. The truth is many good things can be accomplished from technology, but you cannot ignore the obvious: you *do* have to limit the time spent in passive entertainment. You cannot ignore the fact that if your kids are on an iPad or watching television constantly, there is neither time nor inclination for curious wonderings. The trick is to use technology as a servant, not to let it be your master.

Of course, this begins with us setting the example first. You know what you have to do, mama. Time to put down that phone and play with your kids. Set guidelines for your own technology usage and enforce it. Let your kids see you reading, being creative, and ignoring the phone during family time.

THE GIFTS OF HOMESCHOOLING

While absolutely any family can learn and discover together, homeschooling without a doubt has afforded my family the chance to do this more than we would have otherwise. I don't share this to cause anyone undue pressure. I always hold homeschooling with a very open hand, every year prayerfully considering, "Is this right? Is this for us? What do you think, Lord?" I know many kids have positive educational experiences in conventional school environments. I was one of them.

The Gift of Time Together

By the sheer gift of time together, homeschooling has opened doors for us to build memories as a family, and I would be remiss if I didn't suggest it. One thing we do not lack around here is quality time together. Of course, that is more time to poke pencils at each other's kneecaps and dump sand malignantly down one another's shirts. But overall, we have become deep, true friends due to the quality time we spend together.

The Gift of a Second Education

I have received a second education, alongside my kids. Was my first education so dreadfully lacking? Or do I just not remember how stunning the human brain is, how inexplicable men dragging rocks over hundreds of years to make a pyramid? Together, you learn and relearn—delving into books about ancient Greece, tinkering with magnets, relishing great works of children's literature you loved as a child or never had the chance to read.

The Gift of a Free Schedule

I think my favorite thing about the homeschooling schedule is the freedom to direct your own days. Recently I had an appointment and had to leave home at the unholy hour of 7:30 a.m. The act of getting my kids dressed and out the door with their respective possessions nearly undid me. How do you school or working moms do it? I will never know. As a type A personality, I'm surprised how much I love the opportunity and freedom to snuggle on the couch for just a little bit before breakfast, to let the kids keep doing the puzzle they're engaged in, to start an hour later or earlier if we feel like it. And there's no one telling us how or when!

Because we are home so much, it feels like we can fit more into our day. We can sit on a couch under a fuzzy blanket on a Tuesday, just because. We can bake together. We can play checkers. We can make Valentine's Day cards for the neighbors, we can write to our Compassion-sponsored children, we can paint flowers with water-color (and crumple it up when it's just not right and start again). Since I'm just not one of these supermoms (you know who you are) who would fit these things into the margins of the afternoons and weekends, I am grateful for homeschooling. I know my tendencies, and if I had to corral everyone into the car every day with all their appointed clothes and bags and shoes and papers, I would no doubt spend my limited time with them more drill sergeant than mother.

If your family is thinking about homeschooling, consider this a vote in the affirmative from my (albeit distanced) perspective. It may not be a good fit, but it may! I always consoled myself in the deciding years with the assurance that it wouldn't hurt to try it, you know? If you've never tried it, I assure you that homeschooling is every bit as rewarding as you can imagine it to be. It's also every bit as frustrating as you can imagine.

WORDS OF ENCOURAGEMENT FOR ANY MOM WHO HAS TRIED TO TEACH HER KIDS ANYTHING, EVER

Homeschooling is basically a microcosm of parenting. It's all the things about parenting squished together in one massive, swirl-ing pressure-cooker situation for much of the day. Whether you homeschool or not, if you at any point attempt to do some sort of learning project with a child, you will experience a universal fact: it's fun, exasperating, amazing, and every-last-nerve-racking to be deeply involved with your kids and how their brains work.

And as unglamorous as it is, it's the minute-by-minute choices that make good teachers and good mamas. Do I stay stuck on my phone, or shut it down for real life? Do I continue the frantic tidying, or play pretend store with a three-year-old? Do I have that difficult conversation about character when my mind is filled to the brim with a thousand other things? Do I lug everyone to the park for an adventure when spirits are down? Do I do that project, read that book, engage with my child and his friends, over and over again?

There is no magic button to make a happy, enriched home. It is, truthfully, a long repetition of choices made all day long, like storing up acorns in a tree hollow for winter.

Yes, I will read that book.

Yes, I will bake cookies and let you measure it out.

Yes, we can stop and examine this dead worm.

Yes, I'll stay up late so we can talk through your teenage questions (even though I'm exhausted).

Yes, we can listen to your playlist as we prepare dinner and set the table.

Yes, we can set a date to listen to a podcast you like, and the next time, I'll choose one.

Yes, I will read that book. (Again. There is a lot of book reading.)

Yes, I'm turning off my phone/shutting down my computer so we can discuss what happened in class today.

Let us not become weary in learning alongside our kids, even when it is frustrating. It is the good, good work.

THINGS TO CONSIDER

As you brainstorm your own family traditions, here are some things to consider:

- What childhood books have been most meaningful to you?
- When do you currently read together as a family? Can you

think of new rituals that will help you add time reading aloud, or individually, into your day?

- What's one of your passions? What do you love to learn about? How can you share this passion with your kids?
- Can you think of some ways to increase hands-on education in your home? How would each of your kids benefit from time using their hands, whether it's sensory play, exploring, building, creating, or painting?
- Think of one way your family uses technology in a productive way. What is one practice or habit you'd like to limit or eliminate?

SUGGESTED THINGS TO DO

- Make a family bucket list of the field trips you want to go on before your kids leave home. Maybe you want to visit the library monthly, or maybe you have a wild hope to tour the Vatican. Dream big, I say. Make a one-year, five-year, and ten-year plan for knocking these off the list.
- Create a story-time ritual. If you need some good literature suggestions, I recommend the book lists found in *Honey for a Child's Heart* by Gladys Hunt and *The Read-Aloud Family* by Sarah Mackenzie. Make reading a regular part of your day. With younger kids, story time in the afternoon, at bedtime, or after breakfast is a wonderful ritual. For older elementary-aged kids, start a summer reading contest for the family. Before you head on vacation with your teens, start a tradition of visiting the bookstore to get a new book first.
- Cultivate an atmosphere of curiosity. Let me translate this for you into normal mom talk. Let not your heart become weary if someone asks you for the forty-seventh time where

the mommy birdies live, how a walkie-talkie works, or if it's cold enough to snow. Discuss, wonder, and marvel with your kids. Don't be so caught up in your own adult world that you don't talk to your kids about what they are curious about.

- Pack the home with opportunities for fun, educational traditions. For example, work puzzles at Christmas, crosswords on Sundays, or word searches on car rides. Buy a placemat with the states on it, and quiz each other on capitals at mealtimes. Listen to educational podcasts over lunch or breakfast. Play trivia games together. Instead of a silly sitcom, watch documentaries like the Planet Earth series. Have your kids do show-and-tell at dinnertime about one thing they've learned that week. Discuss current-events issues at dinner.

CHAPTER 8

SERVICE

When Someone Needs Help, We Help

Greater love has no one than this, that
someone lay down his life for his friends.

—JESUS[1]

MY FAVORITE THINGS ARE LEISURELY MORNINGS, GOUR-
met food, and poolside naps. But even though June 25, 2003,
included *none* of these things, it is still one of my favorite days.
This was my day as a leader at Lake Champion Young Life Camp
in New York:

- Wake up at 6:30 a.m. in a sweaty sleeping bag with an occupied spiderweb hanging above my bunk bed.
- Spend ninety seconds primping for the day—in other words,
  pulling my hair into a bun and throwing on a T-shirt, sports
  bra, and athletic shorts.
- Gingerly awaken eight high-maintenance, grumpy high school
  girls who would rather still be asleep.

- Scarf down cafeteria-style pancakes and sausage links, having served myself last.
- Pour lukewarm coffee and powdered creamer into a Styrofoam cup, drink two sips, and then accidentally leave it somewhere.
- Spend twelve straight hours listening to Bible talks, reassuring high school girls they look beautiful, defusing their petty fights, and pretending to enjoy mountain biking and freezing-cold lake water.
- For the entire day, don't look in a mirror, sit down to rest, or do one thing I want to do. Instead, follow these girls around wherever they'd like to go, entertaining them, listening to them, and sharing Jesus with them.

That was my day. And when I collapsed into my sleeping bag in the un-air-conditioned cabin at 11:00 p.m., I had literally never been happier. It hardly seems possible, but it's true. I know you've experienced it too. An others-faced life is the most rewarding. It's a paradoxical, unexpected, and upside-down truth of gospel living.

If life is better when we live for others, what does it mean within the family? What does it mean for family traditions? *Some of the best traditions serve others.*

In her wonderful book *What Is a Family?*, Edith Schaeffer says that a family should be "a door that has hinges and a lock."[2] I believe she means two things. On the one hand, a family should regularly close the door to the outside. It's not healthy for a home to have a steady revolving door of parties, events, and guests. A family should make its own memories, have its own alone time, be a designated unit.

At the same time, however, a family is not a sealed box or secluded island. A door with hinges opens to the outside. We go out; we invite people in.

I know this outward emphasis is good. I know it's fulfilling. But to be honest with you, I'm bad at it. Sometimes motherhood is so much. By the time I've cleaned off the kitchen counters for the fifty-third time and put everyone to bed and gotten them each water and scratched each back and said all the prayers, it feels there is nothing left to give.

And when it comes to some types of service, I'm scared. I mean, it's one thing to float one's own self, single and twenty-five years old, down the Amazon River in a canoe delivering Bibles to a Peruvian tribe. Been there, done that on my week-long summer mission trip. But to board that canoe now, with three kids in tow? That's quite another thing. Serving just feels more complicated with kids. I think about my child with food allergies, and the unknown risks seem like too much. I can't tell you how many times I've been so close to volunteering our family to serve, but my worries have left the e-mail unsent, the phone call unmade. I want to have one of those world-changer families, but quite honestly, I like our cozy little family safe inside our home.

> A family that is only about the family is missing out.

But a family that is only about the family is missing out. The Lord reminds me that my clenched-fist way of life isn't safe; it's sad. In fact, C. S. Lewis said:

> Indeed, if we consider the unblushing promises of reward and the staggering nature of rewards promised in the Gospels, it would seem that Our Lord finds our desires not too strong, but too weak. We are half-hearted creatures, fooling about with drink and sex and ambition when infinite joy is offered us, like an ignorant child who wants to go on making mud pies in a slum because he cannot imagine what is meant by the offer of a holiday at the sea. We are far too easily pleased.[3]

See, I have it backward. I sometimes feel in my mixed-up mind that we "have to" serve, but no—we *get* to. Real, deep, abiding joy of the purest kind is hiding just around the corner in our acts of love.

Kristen Welch has lived this. She and her husband sold their home and moved to a smaller one. They scrimped and saved, not for a family vacation but to travel with their children back and forth from Ethiopia, running a nonprofit that gives dignifying work to women in poverty. In her excellent book *Raising World Changers in a Changing World*, Kristen describes what it's been like for her family to sacrifice so much. Spoiler alert: it's been incredible:

> When my husband and I were handed our pink and blue bundles of joy, we didn't plan to raise world changers. But the moment we started teaching them to put others first, we discovered that small acts of kindness and compassion *do* change the world. Mostly, however, they change us.
>
> Honestly, our lives today look nothing like I thought they would. I spent the first half of my married life trying to create a happier life for my family. But instead of feeling satisfied with all that filled our home and hearts, we felt hollow and empty. When we began giving to others, we discovered that we didn't have less for ourselves, we had more. So yes, our lives are different than I planned—*they are better.*[4]

HOW TO BECOME A FAMILY WHO SERVES

You picked up this book looking for practical traditions. More practical tips are coming! But the point is this: we shouldn't read them and think, "I'll never do all this, so I think I'll just quit." Let's throw off any guilt about what we *should do* and imagine all the family adventures and rich joy to be found in serving others.

Make It an Adventure

My friends Amy and Pete celebrate Saint Nicholas Day with their family by "candy caning" someone in need. They sneakily stick a few candy canes in a family's yard one night, then leave an anonymous gift card in the mailbox. What's interesting is how Amy describes it. "The kids get such a rush. They feel like they're being so stealthy, rebellious, and adventurous. It's a blast."[5]

Imagine all the family adventures and rich joy to be found in serving others.

My neighbors Brandon and Emily, when they're doing an act of kindness, tell their kids, "We're going to go be superheroes and make someone smile today."[6] Serving others will naturally bring a sense of joy, so why not play this up?

Let Kids Take the Lead

My cousin's daughter Josephine loves doing crafts, and she came up with the notion to stitch together felt hearts, add essential oils, and sell them as car air fresheners. She raised over three hundred dollars to donate to a local center that houses women and children in times of distress. I love this! Our kids may thoroughly surprise us with their ideas to serve, but it will probably require us to be available to help their dreams come to fruition. Our role is to cast a vision for what it could look like to serve others, to offer input, and to be available for who knows what kinds of errands to make it happen.

If your kids are like mine, you may need to tweak their ideas just a tad. For example, after I talked with my boys about serving, they concocted a plan to construct a giant bike ramp made out of dirt smack in the center of our (finally green) lawn. They planned to charge the neighborhood kids a fee to ride the ramp, and then they'd donate the money to charity. I fortunately caught this plan when the shovels were just breaking ground. Let's just say we went back to the drawing board.

Start Where You Are

Whenever I feel like I need to do something *big* to serve, I'm reminded that we can begin right where we are by loving those whom God has placed in our path already. After I underwent surgery for an ectopic pregnancy, my friend Jean scrubbed my whole house, then sat next to me while I cried.

In college I was heartbroken when my engagement ended. I opened my mailbox to find a note from my cousin. It said, "I am Jessica. I am loved. I am safe. I am everything someone has wanted. I am beautiful . . ." These were people right in my path who showed me God's love when I needed it most.

As the need arises, we should be service ready. I think this is a tradition of its own. Our kids will notice if we have open hearts to serve those who might need us. Often these are the Good Samaritan moments—the opportunities that pop up when we haven't planned for them, when we are on our way somewhere else, but we see someone in need. Here are a few examples:

- You remember it's your widowed neighbor's birthday, so you take a few minutes to stop to buy flowers and a card.
- Someone is sick or has had a baby, so you deliver them dinner.
- You spontaneously do chores for someone who is unable to work.
- You hear of a need somewhere in the world, so you stop and pray.

Yes, these can become family traditions: when someone needs help, we help.

Partner with a Worthy Cause

There are only 5.2 million different places you could serve. It can be overwhelming. To get you started, I'll share three organizations I'm currently aware of that are in great need.

Pen pals with a mission.

Our family sponsors children through Compassion International, which shares the gospel and provides aid to children overseas. We used to be horribly inconsistent at writing to them until I learned they have a letter opening day at most of the centers, and the kids without letters can feel sad. I resolved that very day to become more disciplined about writing. Plus, now that my kids are older, I make them write letters too.

Safe haven for children.

My friends Jeff and Lauren are foster parents. Their phone often rings in the dead of night, and shortly after there's a knock at the door and a little one who needs loving care. Sometimes the need is for twelve hours; sometimes it's for years. They rarely know for sure how long or even why they've been asked to serve.

They answer the call to care for these babies, showering them with love, and then letting them go. I just love the tradition of service their kids are able to witness (and participate in). "It's simultaneously the hardest and most rewarding thing you can do," they said. "And it's work that the church needs to be doing. It isn't for the faint of heart, and you will need a good support system, but if you can—*do it*. You won't regret it, and you and your kids (if you have them) will grow in ways you didn't think possible."[7] Consider fostering or assisting families who foster through an organization called Foster Village, which helps provide meals, supplies, and respite care for these families.

The invisible generation.

Finally, there is a group largely ignored today, even in Christian circles: the elderly. As I shared on my blog, this generation suffers from the misfortune of being unmarketable and out-of-date in our image-based, style-obsessed culture. No one is posting social media styling pics of hospital-gown attire or Instagramming their lonely, cafeteria-style mashed potato dinners. It's just not on trend. Plus, it takes patience to sit and chat with someone who is different from us. (Remember that art? I think we lost it somewhere between the DVR and the iPhone.)

As the Gen X and Gen Y church, we have our trendy ministries, the ones that make good T-shirts and hashtags, ones like parenting, mission trips, refugee aid, adoption, orphan care, and cancer research. Do not misread me—these ministries are absolutely valuable, needed, and laudable. We don't need fewer of these, but we need more. There are so many lonely senior adults; where do we even start? The Bible calls us to care for those inside our families first.[8] If we have aging grandparents, parents, uncles, or aunts, we are called to care for them and meet their needs. From there, we should look to the needs of our neighbors, our church, and the community. Younger kids can make holiday cards or perform their musical instruments for elderly residents in the community; older kids could teach computer skills to older residents and help in their homes or yards as needed.

IDEAS FOR SERVING
THROUGHOUT THE YEAR

As promised, here is a bunch of fun, creative ways to serve throughout the year. Again, don't become overwhelmed by the thought of doing them all or feel like you need to do everything right this second. Pick a few you like and mark them, or browse this list when you get the whim to serve.

January

- Boxing Day. Boxing Day is actually December 26, but this fun tradition seems to meld more thematically with January, so I include it here. This is a British holiday involving a multitude of silly and fun activities, but many people in the US associate the holiday with boxing up things you don't need. The Wray family was prompted by this acquired meaning of the holiday, and my friends created their own tradition. Every year they hold a Boxing Day auction. Everyone from kids to grown-ups brings something they don't want in good condition. They hold an auction, then donate the proceeds to a ministry. It's fun and ministry-minded.
- Dr. Martin Luther King Jr. Day. How about a day of service in Dr. King's honor? Martin Luther King Jr. believed all people deserve to be treated respectfully and kindly. What a fantastic way to honor Dr. King—not just with our words or fanfare but by pouring into our communities, especially those that are typically overlooked or ignored. You could drop off food to a homeless shelter or deliver flowers to a local assisted-living center.
- Blessing Bag Party. Make cold-weather blessing bags for the homeless and keep them in your car. Include snacks, water, hand warmers, hat and gloves, a Bible, medical supplies, and a blanket. Then, hand them out to people in need as you see them during your daily drives.

February

- Super Bowl Soup. Since February is the month the Super Bowl is played, it's a wonderful time to consider volunteering at a soup kitchen. ("Soup-er" bowl, get it?) Or collect soup cans to give to one of your local food banks.

- Valentine's Day Hope. Valentine's Day is a wonderful time to show love, especially to the needy. This can be a particularly discouraging time for those in women's shelters. What about dropping off some beautiful flowers and a home-cooked meal to these ladies?

- Valentines from Mommy. We shouldn't overlook the impact of showing love to our own children. I try to make my own valentine for each one of them, even if it's very simple.

- Sickness Baskets. I always think of February as the month of the flu. Sickness abounds! Take dinner, flowers, coffee, Lysol wipes, or a batch of groceries to a friend whose family is sick. It is absolutely one of the kindest, most appreciated acts of service one can do.

March and April

- Easter Cards for Neighbors. This is a great way to share your Christian faith in a way that is palatable to others. We decorated cards to look like Easter eggs and wrote on them: "Jesus said, 'I am the resurrection and the life.'" Then we delivered them with Morning Glory Muffins to our neighbors.

- Easter Dinner and a Conversation. Easter is a wonderful time to invite friends to church, as many people consider going on Easter Sunday even if they may not regularly attend. Or invite friends for dinner and show a movie about the life of Christ, perhaps the *Jesus* film or *The Passion of the Christ*.[9]

- Nature Cleanup. How about a trail or park cleanup? Use rubber gloves and beautify a favorite area.

- Pi Day Ding Dong Ditch. March 14 is Pi Day. (Pi = 3.14—get it?) How about baking a pie and leaving it as a surprise for a neighbor?

- Arbor Day Tree Planting. Planting a tree is fun and an act of service for future generations.

May

- National Day of Prayer. During May, write down a list of people you can pray for, and have your kids draw one out of a cup and pray for them at breakfast or dinner each day. Then drop a few of these people a note to let them know they've been prayed for.
- Mother's Day Love. Mother's Day can sometimes be a day of disappointment or unmet expectations. Instead of waking up and thinking, *I want a day off!* I have found that I have a much better day by thinking of others, whether it's my own mother, my mother-in-law, those who have lost children or mothers, or those who don't have any children but long to. Ironically, shifting our perspective from *inward* to *outward* makes a huge difference in how we enjoy the day. We can remember these friends by bringing them a flower, sending them a little note, or praying for them.
- Love a Teacher. As a former teacher, I want to say that Teacher Appreciation Day (or week) is a wonderful thing. I still have and treasure the handwritten notes from my students. And I enjoyed those coffee shop gift cards for a long time too. Don't forget the Sunday school teachers who serve your children. These volunteers work tirelessly, often thanklessly, so remember them at the end of the year.
- Memorial Day Moments. Consider volunteering to place flags at a veteran's cemetery.

June

- Father's Day Letters. Many men love words of affirmation. Consider taking the time each year to have each child say or write the things they appreciate about Dad. We made lists of what we admire about both grandpas; one has his framed above his bed, the other carries it in his briefcase everywhere. These words are powerful.

- Family Day of Service. Take a Saturday and serve where you're needed, whether for a neighbor or local organization.

July

- Summer Blessing Bags. Make summer blessing bags to keep in your car for the homeless. Include sunscreen, bottles of water, sunglasses, ChapStick, and other warm-weather must-haves.
- Mission Trip Memories. What a wonderful tradition it would be to serve on a mission trip as a family during the summer. You can choose to do this at a certain milestone, for example, when a child turns sixteen. Or alternate between a family vacation one year and a family mission trip the next.

August

- Natural Disaster Relief. Hurricane season is a good reminder of how we can help during natural disasters. When hurricanes, earthquakes, or other natural disasters hit, it's easy to feel numb or powerless to help. Always do something if you feel convicted. It can be as simple as adding these events to your family prayer time or donating a small amount to trusted organizations. This teaches our families to *interact and act*, not just watch a world crisis unfold.
- Write to a Grandparent. The downtime of the summer months provides an excellent opportunity to practice thoughtfulness (and revive those school skills) in the old-fashioned art of letter writing. Grandparents especially love to receive letters and cards from their grandkids. If your kids don't have a grandparent, have them write to an elderly church or community member.

September

- School Supply Help. Donate a book bag full of school supplies for families in need.
- Bless a Teacher. Bless a teacher in a low-income school by providing classroom supplies or a gift card to purchase things he or she may need for the upcoming year.
- Apple Love. Bake an apple pie or apple cake for a neighbor or elderly friend.

October

- Birdie Love. As it begins to get chilly outside, we love to fill up our birdfeeder and care for the birds. Caring for God's creation is a great act of service.
- Halloween or Harvest Party. No matter what you think of Halloween, you can't deny that there can be a great opportunity for meeting and engaging with your neighbors during this day. In our neighborhood, we have a giant chili dinner block party and redeem the creepy holiday. You could also host a costume parade through a senior center or assisted-living center. A homeschooling group in our area does this, and it is a hit with the residents.

November

- Leaf Raking. What a wonderful way to show love to a neighbor. And the kids enjoy helping out and jumping in the leaves.
- Soup Kitchen Service. Volunteering at a soup kitchen around Thanksgiving is a perfect fit for families looking to serve. The needs are usually great this time of year.
- Honor a Veteran on Veteran's Day. Write a letter to someone in active military service or send a card or make a phone call to a veteran you know and thank him or her for serving.
- Operation Christmas Child. This is one of my favorite service

projects. Stockpile goodies for your boxes all year long, then pray for each child as you send off their box of Christmas cheer to them (drop-off is in mid-November).

December

- Saint Nicholas Day Act of Service. Celebrate Saint Nicholas Day on December 6 by honoring his tradition of giving gifts to needy families. Call your local women's shelter or a ministry to low-income families and ask for a family for which to provide Christmas presents.
- Angel Tree Christmas. Angel Tree is a ministry of Prison Fellowship that provides Christmas presents for children of prisoners on behalf of their incarcerated parents.
- Christmas Card Prayers. As you receive Christmas cards, take time at breakfast or dinner to pray for these friends and family.

In some seasons of life, it may feel as if you don't have much to offer and that even a few of these service projects would take a Herculean effort. But in every season, we can love. Even if it's being a faithful prayer warrior for friends, offering a smile to a neighbor, or opening the door for another customer at the store, a small act of kindness can absolutely make a person's day, just as a grumpy or unkind act can ruin one.

THINGS TO CONSIDER

As you brainstorm your own family traditions, here are some things to consider:

- What memories of serving others stand out to you from your life?

- What are the most memorable times you've served with your kids?
- Do you tend to prefer staying in your home, or is it easy for you to get out and serve?
- Who comes to mind as someone who may be lonely or in need right now?
- What organizations are you passionate about?

SUGGESTED THINGS TO DO

- Write down one way that your family can serve an organization you are passionate about.
- Look over the month-by-month ideas in this chapter and choose three ways to serve throughout the year.
- Make a prayer jar and write the names of people from your job, neighborhood, and family on slips of paper. Draw out one or two names every day and pray for them. Every so often, drop them a note (from you or the kids), and let them know you've prayed for them.
- Sponsor a child with Compassion International. It is an excellent organization that I highly recommend. Already have a sponsored child? Send him or her a note.
- Find a retirement or assisted-living home and send cards or visit occasionally to play games or offer a musical recital.
- Have a secret-servant game every so often. For a whole week, each person in the family is secretly paired with another for whom he or she does kind acts. At the end of the week, reveal who you are.

CHAPTER 9

RELATIONSHIPS

One-on-One Time Makes
the Difference

Rules without relationship leads to rebellion.
—JOSH MCDOWELL[1]

FOR TWELFTH-GRADE WRITING CLASS, I WROTE A POEM called "I Wish Snowmen Never Melted." To my dad, and my dad alone, this poem is a masterpiece. The charge was to write a Christmas poem, and the practical, unimaginative creature that I am, I just typed out my Christmas wishes and called it a day:

> I wish
> that snowmen never melted
> that Santa was real
> that everyone had a mommy like I do
> that every Christmas was a white Christmas
> that every Cinderella always found her Prince Charming.

It was a real literary work of art, as you can see. It actually gets even more cheesy and cliché, so I'll spare you the rest. However, to my dad, I may as well be Emily Dickinson. He's asked me for a copy of this poem at least six times, and twice in college he mailed one back to me along with a gift card for pizza. I think it honestly may be in his briefcase today. He loves this poem because he loves me.

Fast-forward ten years, and that silly poem was the furthest thing from my mind. Gone were the days of snowmen and Christmas wishes; Todd and I were officially adults. Nothing makes you feel more grown-up than knowing *you* are the one responsible to pay stacks of hospital bills and get a crying baby to somehow fall asleep. The crying-baby part, you sort of get better at. The bills—well, they keep coming. The worst part is realizing no matter how frugal you are, no matter how organized your coupon box is, no matter how many times you do and redo the budget, it just might not be enough.

Eight years ago we'd just found out I was pregnant again, and it was suddenly clear the house was too small, the car was too small, and of course, the single income that was already too small would be way too small. We met in our living room with some "very helpful" financial advisers, who showed us color-coded charts explaining that in addition to the $1.3 million we'd need for retirement (yes), we'd better save a total of $394,000 for our two children's college educations. Charts are usually comforting to visual types like me, but these made me want to throw up and hide my stupid coupon box with those silly two-dollar Pampers coupons.

As if on cue, my car started making a humming noise. *An expensive humming nois*e. I think there was a lump in my throat when I reported the damage back to Dad, the resident car expert. "I need a new hubcap system. It's $449, but it's okay. It could be worse."

"You take Visa?" I impatiently asked the cashier at the mechanic's office a few days later, eager to swipe and forget. Then came the words you hear in movies, or in other people's stories.

"It's been taken care of."

I looked up. "What? By who?"

"A very nice gentleman came in here and wanted to take care of it."

And he handed me the receipt. My eyes blurred with tears, but something was circled, and in between all the random numbers and car jargon was a phrase so out of place but so familiar: "The snowman never melted."

Dad.

He'd gone into the mechanic shop sometime during the week and paid the bill.

This story embodies so much of what I love about my dad. He never tires of finding sneaky ways to show us that we are loved. It's not about money, of course, although I will tell you straight up that the $449 gift might as well have been $4.4 million at that juncture. No, more often with Dad, it's something small—a text, a phone call, a dropped-off Starbucks on a lonely cold winter morning. Little acts to poke in our lives with the reminder we are noticed, special, and loved.

This is the clincher in the whole thing about memory-making: we need ways to tell our children, "*You matter.*" You, individually. My parents weren't perfect in raising us four kids (no one is), but somehow we all felt that we were their favorite.

As parents, and especially as mamas, we can become laser focused on running all the things in the family. (And a good thing too—that toilet paper isn't going to buy itself.) We have a show to run. We have places to go, lists to check, memories to make. And then there are the values and truth we want to impart. But we must consider: If the well-oiled machine of the family is running but its members don't feel loved, then what good is it? Have we really accomplished anything without love?

My friend Bill, when recalling his difficult childhood, comments, "My brother was basically invisible in our family. He was the middle child, and he somewhat blended into the background."[2] My heart breaks when I hear this. And my resolve deepens that each of my kids would be known and loved, not feeling like they're tagalongs to someone's agenda but valued members of our family.

This chapter on individual bonding is essential. There are sundry ways to do it, but some way, somehow, that rich point of connection needs to happen.

The whole idea sounds great in theory, but it is costly. Its price is the most expensive commodity we own: time.

Here I am preaching this very thing, and to be totally honest with you, it has been hard for me to do this regularly. We're no different from your family, I imagine. My husband works long hours during the week, and between homeschooling, managing the home, and writing on the side, life is busy. Throw in a sports season or two, add a few birthday parties or church events, and it starts to feel like it's just not worth it to add yet another activity, like a mommy-son date, to the family schedule.

> If the well-oiled machine of the family is running but its members don't feel loved, then what good is it?

Maybe this chapter feels like the final straw for your already-burdened load. *You're telling me we have to celebrate the birthdays, and the holidays, and go on adventures, and now this? One-on-one time too?* Sweet mama, I want to reassure you with two things:

1. It doesn't need to be frequent, so long as it happens.
2. You're probably doing it more than you realize.

THE GIFT OF ONE-ON-ONE TIME

Hold my hand as we think about what this could look like for your family. Because really, one-on-one time is so worth it. These traditions may be some of your kids' most treasured memories. Recently, my husband took our three-year-old daughter on a date. She counted down the weeks beforehand and told no fewer than 156 people that she was going on a date with her daddy. As we were getting ready—she wanted to wear her special red dress with gold hearts, of course—she told me, "Mommy, I like going on dates with Daddy because he's my daddy and I love him." An exact quote. (Can you please stay like this forever, sweet girl?)

This one-on-one time is something that grandparents, aunts, or uncles can easily implement as well. I have a single friend who is an absolutely wonderful aunt to her little nieces and nephews. She considers her role as aunt to be of utmost importance. When the kids have their birthdays, they always get to go on a special date with Aunt Elizabeth. My mom tries to take each of her grand-kids on dates with Grammy. They may go to the dollar store, to Chick-fil-A for a milkshake, or just to swing at the park. With more than a dozen little ones, it's a long wait between turns, but they treasure this tradition so much. Again and again, the return on these investments has far outweighed the cost of time or effort on our part.

These dates don't need to be expensive or official either. It can be as simple as throwing a little one in the car seat in the back of the truck while you go to Lowe's to get light bulbs. My daughter is three and loves to go grocery shopping with me. There are lots of times it would be much easier to make a weekend grocery run alone, but it brings her such joy to tag along with Mommy. She chatters the entire time we're driving, and she loves to help me fetch the bananas and sample all the treats on display. Of course,

I do go alone sometimes, but if I get that little nudge that maybe I should take her, I try to do that.

I've heard so many stories of parents who have a special thing they do *only* with a particular child. Maybe one child in your home loves fishing and the other, board games. Maybe you talk theology with one kid and sports scores with the next.

My cousin, who adopted a son who is African American, has implemented one ritual uniquely suited to him. She explains, "Hair and its care is a big part of black culture, so I drive thirty minutes to take him to a black barbershop that was recommended to me. I want him to (a) not miss out on that experience, (b) have an opportunity to learn about these things directly from other black males, and (c) be able to walk into one as an adult and feel like he's not an outsider."[3] I love her efforts to uniquely parent this child.

It can be difficult to make sure everyone gets quality time when you have a large household of kids. My friend Liesel is mom to five children, and she devised a plan to spend some special time with each child. Every so often they allow just one child to stay up late with the parents. The child gets to choose what they'd like to do: a game, craft, whatever. Then Liesel and her husband, Mark, ask the child if he or she has a prayer request, and they pray together. My friend noted that it's amazing how each child comes alive during these special times.[4]

TIPS FOR MAXIMIZING DATES
WITH YOUR CHILD

As you envision your one-on-one time with each child, here are a few guiding principles to consider.

Choose How to Make Date Nights a Tradition

Date nights can be frequent or infrequent. Becky, the creator of *Your Modern Family*, suggests a monthly date night for each child on the same date he or she was born.[5] For example, my son was born March 3, so the third of every month would be his special date night.

In our family we divide up the months of the year and let each child have a month. They each get their birthday months—we often skip December or other typically busy months—and scatter out the rest. They get one date during their month.

Talk It Up

Whatever the frequency of your dates with your kids, maximize the time by talking up the day as it approaches. Then after it's over, remember what you did together. In this way you make it last that much longer. "Remember that day we went to the play together, and then had hamburgers, just us? Wasn't that awesome? What should we do this year?" So much of the treasure of traditions is the looking-forward-to and the reminiscing afterward.

Put the Phone Down

I am fortunate enough to be a member of the last generation who remembers what it was like to ride in the family minivan without being disrupted by the nagging urge to check my e-mail. I remember an era of vacation where there was absolutely no obligation to tweet, post, or share. (I mean, really. Did our honeymoon *actually even happen* if Facebook was not alerted? It hardly seems possible.)

Yes, the iPhone may have given us the ability to order a pair of jeans at a stoplight, but it also took something from us. We lost meaningless conversation. Yes, meaning*less*. Sure, we still talk.

But that time—the time we now spend crouched over our phones, scrolling—that space used to be filled with something else. It was ambling, careless, comfortable nothing-talk that's the stuff real relationships are made of. When you've gone to the trouble to be with just one child for a snatch of time, or when somehow the stars align and you have been gifted with the rare blessing of some time together, even if it's for a doctor's visit or waiting for another child or whatever, then make that time count. Put the phone down. Let yourself be bored, together. Let there be empty, thoughtful silence. Let them know they are most important.

The other day I was at a sandwich shop seated next to what I presume was a mother and her preteen daughter. During the entire meal, the mom was pecking away on her phone while her daughter silently forked through her salad. Of course, I don't know what this mom was doing on her phone, and perhaps there was a matter of true urgency that needed to be handled. But this pattern can be observed everywhere. I shudder to think how many times I have done it myself. We must fight it, mamas. This is a fight that will never go away, and it is worth all the effort it takes and then some. Relationships over technology.[6]

THE GIFT OF BIRTHDAYS

Birthdays are the ideal opportunity to make a child feel special. They're the best day of the year to a kid! My sweet girl's birthday is in August, and literally since September of last year, she has been reminding us that she will have a princess birthday party on her birthday. For eleven whole months, she's been imagining the dress she'll wear, the cake she'll have, the guests who will come. And it's not just a girl thing; my son had his football party planned for a good half a year too.

Birthdays are important to our kids; therefore, they should be important to us. At the same time, my goodness! Can I say that birthday parties have gotten completely out of control? Recently I searched for "kids birthday party ideas" on Pinterest. Immediately I found how-to tutorials for: marshmallow tutus, cardboard boxes transformed into life-size go-karts, cupcakes in seven varying shades of green to form the very hungry caterpillar from Eric Carle's book, and a technique to turn a watermelon into a monstrous dinosaur (that was, quite honestly, terrifying).

I am absolutely not saying it's wrong to enjoy throwing a birthday party for your child. If your child has his heart set on a Spider-Man cake, I think it's a wonderful thing to oblige. My sister-in-law Helen should really be a professional party planner, as one of her hobbies is planning beautifully themed parties. If you excel in this arena of homemaking, by all means, use your gifts to bless your family.

But check your motives. We shouldn't feel like we have failed if we don't go to elaborate lengths to throw the "perfect" birthday party with every excessive detail on point, especially if our children are too young to remember or too overstimulated to enjoy it. We should absolutely use children's birthdays to show them love, whatever that looks like.

For one child of mine, it meant calling the city garbage service (yes) to have the garbage truck show up to the party and dump some pretend garbage. For my nephew, it meant enjoying a night out at a Japanese steakhouse restaurant and seeing hibachi steak cooked tableside. For my two-year-old daughter, it meant inviting over all the little girls she knows for a get-dressed-up tea party lunch.

Instead of feeling like we must measure up to society's standards for a birthday, let's go back to the basics and think, *How can*

I love this particular child for one day of the year? What would your particular child enjoy? If he is an introvert, a special dinner out with just Mom and Dad or one friend might mean the world. If she loves animals more than anything, a Saturday at the zoo may be a dream. Is her favorite dessert ice cream sundaes? Would he treasure an afternoon playing golf with Dad?

My brother-in-law Dan said he treasured his birthday dinners growing up. "Every year on our birthdays, my brothers and I got to choose what the family would eat for dinner. I'm sure millions of people do that, but we were fairly regular in our meals so getting to choose was something really exciting."[7] Choosing dinner—how simple is that? And my brother-in-law treasures these memories thirty years later.

Every year John Piper writes each child a poem on his or her birthday. Maybe you aren't poetic (I can relate!), but what about a handwritten note? A family I know writes each child a letter in a special birthday journal, which they read, and Mom and Dad save the journals to give to them on their eighteenth birthdays. Another option is to give the journals at each child's high school graduation. Family members can also speak words of love and appreciation to the birthday child. Here are a few additional ideas for birthday traditions:

- Fill your child's room with balloons or streamers for a morning surprise.
- Let the birthday kid have donuts or cake for breakfast.
- Have the table decorated at breakfast with gifts and share words of blessing. ("What I love about you is . . .")[8]
- Birthday boy or girl gets to go on a special date with Mom or Dad during that month.
- Daughters get the number of roses for their age from their daddy.

THE GIFT OF CELEBRATING MILESTONES WITH YOUR CHILDREN

The magic of milestone birthdays is that you can choose the ones that are important to you. It's a great way to generate excitement over coming events and to recognize your child maturing. Following are just a few suggestions for milestone birthdays:

- a special date before a child begins kindergarten
- a camping trip when a child turns eight
- an overnight trip with Mom or Dad when a child turns ten (I have two friends who took their newly ten-year-old daughters to New York City over Christmas. How magical!)
- a fancy dinner out with Dad and Mom when a child turns thirteen
- a mission trip with Mom or Dad when a child is sixteen
- a trip to Europe or to another country with one parent when a child graduates from high school
- the opportunity for your child to have his or her ears pierced, go hunting, receive a purity ring, or other milestones your family would like to wait until a certain age to honor

My friend Amy and her husband, Pete, instituted a unique program to highlight the rite of passage of their boys into adulthood. They took what they learned and turned it into a fabulous program called Gateway, designed for boys aged eleven to fourteen, to celebrate a boy's induction into manhood. It's a year-long program that is skills based (fishing, hunting, building, and so forth) and also has a spiritual component. Twice a month, a group of these boys get together with their dads to hear from a speaker and learn about a skill. They might learn how to change a tire and then hear a talk about purity in dating, for example. Throughout the year they're recognized for reaching milestones, such as memorizing Scripture or completing a challenging hike.[9]

I love this example of families proactively celebrating the growth of their kids, and, of course, it can be adapted to both genders. While we are busy and occupied, childhood drones on and is gone in a snap. I think the important thing is to interrupt life and speak into our children. It takes intentional planning to tell our kids we are proud of them and that we believe the Lord has a plan for their future.

THE GIFT OF UNDERSTANDING EACH CHILD

We've talked about one-on-one time, being present with our kids, and being strategic about birthdays. But it's also vitally important to learn what each child values, to take time to understand their individual personalities, and to figure out what makes him or her tick. If you love a child with special needs, I know that this may involve a particular challenge as you strive to understand how their little minds work and how to love them best.

In Rachel Jankovic's gem of a book *Loving the Little Years: Motherhood in the Trenches*, there is a chapter called "See Your Children." She talks about the importance of asking yourself questions such as, What is life like for my child? What is it like to be this child on a day-to-day basis? Does this child love to paint more than anything else, but Mom hates messes? Is this child constantly in the shadow of another child?[10]

These words were riveting for me. As I read the book, I was struggling with one of our kids. This child seemed angry at life, and I had no clue why. Following Rachel's prompting, I spent some time imagining what life was like for this child. It was so powerful I choked back tears.

I didn't relinquish disciplining this child for some of the behavioral patterns we were seeing—something we are tempted to do when we feel guilty about a failure to love our kids well. While we disciplined and worked with him, we also worked very hard to understand and connect with him. I observed, really noticed (for the first time, perhaps) what made him frustrated, proud, or stressed. I realized he needed alone time, a snack in the afternoon, to be asked questions he knew the answers to. I saw little things I had missed. He loved cats and dogs, his back being scratched at night, playing games, making little cards for friends. As I poured into this child in the ways that he was needing, he became happier.

And there is something else powerful we cannot overlook: prayers for wisdom in relating to each child. God knows our children. (He made them!) If we are struggling to understand or deal with a child or if it's a difficult season relating to him or her, we can lean on our heavenly Father for patience and wisdom.

THE GIFT OF SHARED CONNECTIONS

It's important to look for a point of connection you can share with each child. Look for something that you both might enjoy doing together. My parents did a good job at this with their four kids. At one point my sister Julie and my mom became very close because they loved cooking shows and home decorating. I couldn't keep the pace on those subjects, and I commented to my sister that I felt left out. She said, "Jessica, we each have our special things with Mom. She and Jenny love helping people. She and John play games together. And you and Mom talk about politics and books." I remember thinking, *She's right!* Both of my parents worked hard to connect with each of us. (And if you're following along, yes, we all have J names!)

A friend shared that, for a while, her husband struggled to find common ground with one of their daughters. "So," she says, "he decided to take up what she loved: musical theater. They attended one event together and found a great connection. They decided to go see more shows together (local high school productions) and to this day still talk about those shows and their nights out together."

THE MOST IMPORTANT
FAMILY RELATIONSHIP

You've probably heard the adage "A healthy marriage is the best gift you can give your kids." I don't know whether it is truly "the best gift," but I know it makes a world of difference, since a family that is entirely kid-centric is not healthy.

If you are married, it makes sense to prioritize memory-making as a couple too. Indeed, while family car trips with several dozen rounds of "Old McDonald Had a Farm" have their own sort of shared specialness between the two of you, it's nice to throw in a few adult-only traditions—you know, just for the heck of it. And maybe to help remind you of why you got together in the first place! My husband and I have a whole host of traditions that we share, and the overflow of the times we share together is a gift to our kids.

Now that our kids are sleeping and eating independently, we usually go away for the weekend for our anniversary, even if it is to the downtown area that is a mere fifteen miles from us. As it turns out, when you're in the thick of raising kids, it doesn't take Bermuda to let you relax. Give me a hotel room and people who make all my meals, and I am in heaven. (We all know the tender spot I have for well-done breakfast buffets.) And let's all take a moment of silent gratitude for grandparents and aunts and uncles who are willing to let their houses be overrun with extra children for several days. *Amen.*

I wish I could tell you that our other marriage traditions involve rock climbing and running marathons together. We are still sort of in the stage where life itself feels like its own version of mountains and marathons, so our traditions are lame and involve take-out Mexican food and watching our special show together every night. Does it make it sound better if I tell you we pray together before we start up Netflix? A little?

And lest you think of us as a super-spiritual couple, I should tell you that this evening prayer tradition started by my saying something very demure and sweet like, "Todd! We *never ever* pray together! Don't you even care about our family's spiritual life?!?" Or something subtle like that. Turns out, my husband would love to pray together, and he was grateful I asked. (Did I mention I have a very patient husband?) This would probably be a good juncture to suggest that if you would like some marital traditions, faith-based or otherwise, just ask. As one who clearly excels in the art of subtle suggesting, I can tell you that it's never too late to just start a new tradition. No need to get all hot and bothered about it; just suggest it. I think there is usually one person in the marriage who tends to be the planner, the organizer, the visionary. That is okay.

I have always thought that Aunt Jamee and Uncle Jerry did a good job celebrating their marriage, so I asked my aunt for some ideas. She said that just because you might schedule some marriage traditions (say, ahem, some that specifically occur in the bedroom) that doesn't make them routine or unromantic. Making regular times to connect—in every way—is beneficial.

She also emphasized the value of traditions that involve your history together. For example, Uncle Jerry took off the first few days of March Madness for the two of them to hole up in a hotel room eating room service and watching basketball for hours on end. This connected them to when they first met, when he was on the team and she was a stat girl.

RELATIONSHIP: THE FOUNDATION FOR EVERYTHING

For my first job out of college, I taught middle school Bible. I still remember the first day I taught a class of real, live kids. I stood at the doorway shell-shocked, thinking, *This cannot be happening. I am not old enough to do this!* Three eighth-grade boys were, despite my new wedge sandals, at least half a foot taller than me. Two of the girls were giggling and passing notes. I wanted to disappear into the tile cracks. I tried clearing my throat a few times, but no one listened. Oh, it was awful! I had clearly made a horrible mistake thinking I could be a teacher! I'm sure my unease was obvious (and comical), though I eventually worked out the kinks and went on to become a fine teacher.

One year the teachers attended a training convention. I remember nothing from this conference except for one statement—one single sentence that became the priceless nugget that paid for the event twelve times over. The speaker made use of a famous quote often attributed to Theodore Roosevelt and said, "Your students won't care how much you know, if they don't know how much you care." Could anything be more trite or cheesy? Yet the truth of that statement has stuck with me throughout half a dozen years of teaching school and a decade of parenting.

Think back. We all had those teachers, didn't we? The ones for whom we were merely a line in the grade book, a warm body in a chair, or a number on a roster. It's likely you don't even remember all of these teachers' names, because it was a mere academic transaction for everyone involved. Unmemorable, efficient, professional.

And then you probably had those few, wonderful teachers who cared about *you*.

The other day I was digging around in my keepsakes box and found the most precious letter from my first-grade teacher, Mrs. Stevenson.

"Dear Jessica," it read in perfect penmanship. "I'm so sorry you are sick today. I hope you feel better. Love, Mrs. Stevenson." It had a little apple drawn below her name and a perfectly round smiley face.

Even as a six-year-old, I knew this homework cover letter was special, and I had to save it. Sweet Mrs. Stevenson loved me. I knew she did. I wasn't just any old first grader. I was Jessica, a homesick newbie who cried for her mommy every single day until January. (Yes. Yes, I did.) I was Jessica, the girl who needed her pigtails adjusted after lunch, who made a beautiful lowercase *g*, who had a beloved sheep puppet at home, who loved when it was her turn to read aloud. This woman knew *me*, loved me.

> They don't care how much you know, unless they know how much you care.

It doesn't matter if you're a teacher, a grandma, a parent, or a boss, the principle stands. To make an impact, we must make a connection. They don't care how much you know, unless they know how much you care.

THINGS TO CONSIDER

As you brainstorm your own family traditions, here are some things to consider:

- Did you feel connected to both of your parents as a child? What special memories do you have with them?

- Think about each of your children's personalities and consider what would make their next birthday special, even if it's unconventional.
- Do you have a child with whom you are struggling to share a connection? What is something you might enjoy doing together?
- Consider your phone habits. Is there a need for you to change some of these to better engage with your family?
- If you are married, what marriage traditions do you currently have?

SUGGESTED THINGS TO DO

- If you have a child with whom you are struggling to connect, spend some time imagining what life is like for that child by "walking in their shoes."
- Determine how you could make dating your kids a regular thing.
- Consider implementing the stay-up-late tradition, where each child gets his or her own special time with Mom and Dad at night.
- Choose two ways you could celebrate special birthday milestones with your children.
- If you're married, think of a yearly tradition for just the two of you.

CHAPTER 10

WORK

The Best Memories Involve Soap and Buckets (More or Less)

I don't pity any man who does hard work worth doing.
I admire him. I pity the creature who doesn't work.

—THEODORE ROOSEVELT[1]

IN CASE ANYONE'S BEEN WONDERING, WRITING A BOOK while homeschooling, running a household, and trying to make memories with your own kids so you're not a memory-making hypocrite is not an easy feat. Shout-out to my wonderful husband and family for giving me space and time so this thing could actually get done. No matter who you are, in busy seasons, something's gotta give. Do you want to know what suffered in our home during this particular season? The stuff in this chapter.

During my writing crunch time, the structure and order in our home disintegrated notably. Daily chores? *Ha!* Clear expectations and firm consequences? *Yeah, right!* I knew we desperately needed more structure, but I lacked a plan. I'd inwardly groan over the unmade beds, the uncleaned messes, and the discarded shreds of craft paper trailing through the living room. I'd think, *You just wait, kids. You just wait till this book is done, and we are getting some* order *around here!*

About this time my friend Katie mentioned a new system that she called "Regaining Order in the Home." I immediately thought, *Now,* that *is what I need!* Katie's system involved three things:

1. Clearly define what is expected in your home for behavior and chores.
2. Come up with easy-to-implement consequences.
3. Create opportunities for kids to earn "chips" to redeem for fun things.

It was exactly what we had been needing, but first I took time to simmer the idea in my head and decide how we'd make it our own. I gradually made a mental list of the things that were annoying me. Everything from "arguing with Mom or Dad," to "leaving your dirty socks all over the place," to "burping at the kitchen table."

I made clear rules about what was expected. Then I made a list of consequences and threw them in a jar. They were color-coded according to the category of infraction, and my husband definitely looked at me like I was a three-headed alien from Neptune when I explained this (but I think he is secretly thrilled he is married to his exact foil). After a week we both agreed: this system was an answer to prayer. No more stressing out about a good punishment or asking-slash-yelling fifty-seven times for people to put their shoes on. Now it was simple to enforce our household rules; when an infraction occurred, I simply pulled a consequence out of the jar.

The final element to this system was the personalized Smartt Chip earning system. The kids could do extra jobs to earn chips and pay for fun things. Just today, the boys redeemed fifteen chips for a morning of fishing with Dad. This structure is what the whole family was needing. It is so surprising to me how the kids have flourished. They have told us they love our new system. Even though they are doing more work than before, they are much happier. *Isn't that something?*

There are two big lessons here for the Mom at Large:

1. Lesson #1: Everyone has stressful seasons when the home turns into a zoo. Instead of getting all weepy that you're a shadow of the mother you hoped you'd be, skip the drama and make a mental list of what you want to change when you have the bandwidth to do so.
2. Lesson #2: Homes run best with clear routines, responsibilities, and chores.

Yes, kids and families *need* work. When you breezed over the table of contents, you may have thought, *Jessica, a chapter on work? Really? How does that fit into a book on celebrating traditions as a family?* I admit, most kids aren't counting down the hours until the next Saturday chore session. No one's favorite summer tradition is the annual flowerbed-weeding session. No one's framing pictures of the minivan deep clean. Work traditions aren't the same kind of fun as a family vacation to the Grand Canyon, but if a home is all festivities and adventures, it's a lopsided picture. Family work should be a planned-for tradition. Here's why.

WHY WORK MATTERS

As adults, we intrinsically know that work is good. But *why*, exactly? It's good to have a few of these reasons in our back pockets in case we face resistance (also known as "whining") when we implement new routines.

Work Makes Us Feel Good

Work is a powerful force in a person's life. At the risk of sounding like a mom on a tirade: the things we value most are the ones we have worked for. If our kids never work really hard at something, they've missed out on a great feeling. When I started my blog, I installed a small ad on my sidebar. I would watch my earnings come in to the tune of about seventeen cents a month. Over the years, my readership grew enough that I could begin making income via ads and sponsorship with small companies. As I invested more and more time, really working at it, the revenue increased. (Did I mention this took *years*? I am not one of those people to ask about quick-earning blogs!)

One day I realized I had earned enough money to purchase a new Apple computer for myself through a big-box store special. I have had nice things before, but this felt entirely different. I had worked, hour on hour, post after post, throughout the late-night hours, to earn this money. What have you been able to achieve, give, or purchase because of your hard work? There is nothing like that feeling, is there?

We experience it in many ways as adults, whether it's finally getting our taxes done, cleaning out that cluttered attic space, or running a race we've been training for. We intrinsically understand that a job well done is rewarding. That feeling is pride. *Pride* has accumulated its share of icky feelings and downward stares. But at its root it's a good thing. We all long for a purpose. My eighty-nine-year-old Grammy may have lost the steadiness in her step, some dexterity, and a good bit of her memory, but one thing remains: her deep, deep need to be useful. Nothing brings her as much joy as folding a big old load of towels, wiping the table, or helping someone with a little task. It's worth working toward; our kids deserve this feeling too.

Work Benefits the Family

Of course, it's not just about the warm and fuzzy feelings *we* get that make work worthwhile. Kids who know how to work are a gift to their families. It's harder to appreciate today, because very few of us live on homesteads where our meals and livelihood depend on how well someone harvested the wheat or milked the cows. But older children are capable of helping to shoulder the growing stresses of the modern family. Teens can handle the lawn care, communicate with the electric company, pick up air filters, teach younger children their letters, iron the church clothes, take the car to get inspected, and on and on. I know of families who experienced financial crisis, and their children stepped up in a big way. They handed over babysitting and house-cleaning money without question to pay for diapers and water bills. It's inspiring how children can rise to the occasion when needed.

Sadly, I more often observe the opposite pattern. Many teenagers are completely preoccupied with their own sports or activities. Parents are run ragged from keeping these activities going, and they simultaneously feel stressed about managing the home. This should not be! The family is a team.

Work Is Glorifying to God

Most of all, work that is well done is glorifying to God. Once in a while I've paid a lady from our community to help clean my house. She is a Russian immigrant who is also a Christian. She told me one time, "Jessica, I clean for God," while she pointed upward. The first time she cleaned my house, I was really moved. I know that sounds weird, but I could almost tell by looking at her work that she was a Christian who cared what God thought of her work. Her work was excellent. She would take the time to line up my daughter's little stuffed animals on her bed. She'd scrub and scrub at some impossibly hard-to-remove stain until it was gone. Everything gleamed and sparkled down to the corners of the closets. Her work inspired me to consider how I can be excellent at my own work. We can teach our kids that God is pleased with excellence.[2]

FOR THE MOMS WHO STRUGGLE TO GET THEIR KIDS TO WORK

I want you to know that I am preaching this message of work to myself too. It's forever something with which I struggle. I tend to do it all so I know that it's *done right*. I am guilty of barking cleaning orders like a drill sergeant. Mostly, I fail to prioritize real work in our kids' lives because we are busy doing everything else. But this tendency, prevalent in my generation, has been to our detriment.

As I explained in a blog post about kids and work, I learned this lesson early on in parenting. One day when my boys were five and three, they were driving me absolutely *crazy*. They'd pulled diapers over their heads and were jabbering like babies. (Pretend baby talk = the worst.) I couldn't get them to listen to a word I said. "Mom," I begged over the phone, "You have to help. These kids are being awful. I have no idea what to do with them!"

"Oh, I was thinking about this, Jessica. They need some sandpaper. That's what."

Sandpaper?

"Yes. Doesn't Todd have any? I'm sure you have some in the garage. Go get them some sandpaper. Take them out on the porch, and just make them sand the porch, the whole thing. You guys should really redo that, anyways."

What in the world? These children were nearly driving me to an early grave with their sinfulness, and this dear woman suggests a porch makeover? It took a few weeks of this, actually. Me: "They're naughty!" Mom: "They need jobs!"

Finally, I gave it a try. It was the day the boys had partitioned the kitchen chairs in the living room in an apparent rendition of a Star Wars episode no one has seen. They were arguing over who was the controller and hammering each other with the rails of said chairs. I walked over, nonchalantly as I could, and ordered, "Guys, I need you to help me wash these windows."

Of course, they looked at me like I was Darth Vader incarnate in the kitchen. But can I tell you that the most magical thing happened? They *did* wash the windows. And furthermore, can I dare to admit what resulted a mere twenty minutes, seventy-five rags, and three gallons of vinegar water later? They were happy! Not "I got that toy from Target" happy. It was a different thing altogether. They were genuinely proud, calm, focused, and well behaved for a good chunk of time afterward. It was eerily successful.

Not one to draw unfounded conclusions, I tried it again with a chore to wipe down the woodwork. The same mystical transformation, from thumb-twiddling little hellions to smiling, peaceful human beings. I have now performed this experiment over and over, and I can assure you it's true. *Work.* Even as little ones, they needed work.

But it's just so much easier for me to do it myself, you may be thinking. No kidding. But try it once. Watch them be occupied happily for thirty minutes, working. See their little faces when they're done. Watch how the house transforms into a heavenly den of structure and order. It's glorious!

Stephen Covey shares the story of a farmer who involved his boys in his work of buying cows. A neighbor stopped by and criticized the boys' work. The farmer's reply: "You don't understand. I'm not raising cows; I'm raising boys."[3]

This phrase has since reverberated in my thoughts, mom-style.

I'm not doing laundry; *I'm raising kids.*

I'm not cleaning windows; *I'm raising kids.*

HOW TO LEVERAGE WORK IN THE FAMILY

So you're convinced good, hard work is just the thing. What next? I have a few tips and tricks to weave work into your family fabric.

Begin Early

Even toddlers can have chore routines. After I published my blog post, "Think You Have Bored Kids? No, Your Kids Aren't Bored—They're Lazy," I had dozens of moms write me to ask, "When can I start?"[4] The answer is now. So often I think of my kids as younger than they really are. I'd be visiting Mom's with one of my babies, and she'd say, "I think this child is ready for a high chair." I'd exclaim, "I just birthed this child! He is an infant!" Lo and behold, guess who was not only capable but thrilled to reach this milestone?

My sweet little daughter was just barely two years old one chore day when she ran to me, gushing, "My room clean!" Sure enough, she had dumped all her things into her baskets and even attempted to pull the covers up on her bed. I was shocked. I hadn't even thought to give her little jobs while we were all working. Very small children can learn to put blocks back in the box, bring a diaper to Mommy, or carry their plate to the sink. I have found the problem is not them, but us. It takes *our* time to train them, to pause from our busyness and involve them in the work.

Model, Model, Model!

If you don't explain exactly what you want, you may end up with a dead plant from zealous overwatering. (Said with experience.) My dad, a business manager, says, "You can't *expect* what you don't *inspect*." In mom talk, this means don't give them fifteen chores, walk away, and get mad if they're not done perfectly! It's a slow and steady walk of showing, teaching, and trying again.

My mother-in-law worked as a Montessori preschool teacher, and she shared with me this neat process for teaching a skill:

> At our school we had a center for learning simple skills like pouring liquid, sweeping a floor, washing dishes, and other household skills. We had to sit with the child first and demonstrate how to do the skill. We didn't talk to explain it, but showed them in small steps what to do. Then we gave them the opportunity to try it. If they didn't seem to get it, we demonstrated again. Often when you tell a child what you want done, they have in their mind what you are saying, but it may not be what you are expecting. Demonstrating is a big help.[5]

Choose Jobs That Are Actually Helpful

At first, I felt like I had to create the *perfect* chart with the *perfect* chore for each child. What a drain! Now, when I get that inkling that the kids need a job, I ask myself, *Self, what do I need done?* Usually self can come up with 379 jobs that need to be done, so I pick the first one, imagining something they could do that *actually* would be helpful to me. Am I making lunches? Have them get out ingredients. Washing dishes? Make them dry. Floor crusty and dirty under my feet? Get the broom! Everyone works together to run the household.

Bye, Bye, Drill Sergeant

It is hard for me to be cheerful when I'm on a mission. Yet it's so very important to be kind and cheery—even when you are rushed, even when you are frustrated, even when they aren't doing it "right." I have the best mother in the world, but somehow I've retained a vivid childhood memory of the time I used way too much cleaner on the bathroom sink. I can still today see Mom's face, her disbelief that felt like her utter disapproval. *All the positive memories of my childhood, and I still feel this one in my bones at thirty-six?*

Of course, my psyche is not scarred, and I survived just fine. But this is a noteworthy testament to how vulnerable we are to criticism. I was really trying to clean the bathroom right; I just didn't know how. Unfortunately, for all the times my own mother expressed her disapproval, I probably express my own four times as much. It is so terribly important that we remember to be kind, gentle, and encouraging as our children are working.

Share Your Stress

It is the weirdest phenomenon. Moms today are overworked and Pinterest-pressured to run manicured houses and produce gourmet-looking meals, yet we also feel obligated to be the sole manager of a steady stream of activities. Now, you know I am a firm believer in making memories . . . obviously! But this work at home should be done together too. Getting the family ready for a trip to the zoo? Put someone in charge of filling the water bottles. Packing for the beach? Instead of letting the kids, say, use afghans to parachute off the couch, let *them* unload the dishwasher, fold the clothes, and pack suitcases. Do not feel like *you* are the one who must single-handedly produce the family fun. Let your kids help you, especially when you are overwhelmed.

Expect Much

As you choose your work routines, consider the amount of work you think your kids can do at their current stage. *Then double it.* Kids are capable of far more than we give them credit for.

Perhaps I lean a tad overboard in my nostalgia for the pioneer era, but I simply cannot lose my admiration for the tremendous amount of work that our ancestors did. As we read Laura Ingalls Wilder's *Farmer Boy* together as a family, we marvel at Almanzo Wilder getting up before dawn in negative thirty degrees (this is not an exaggeration) to milk the cows and get them fresh hay. We are amazed when we read that he lived self-sufficiently at age seventeen, and furthermore embarked on a tremendously brave mission across a roaring blizzard to obtain grain for their starving little Midwestern town. How was he able to do such a feat? His mind, body, and soul had been core-strengthened after a childhood of believing that he could be trusted to do real adult work.

Almanzo Wilder was not an anomaly. A few centuries ago in early American colonies, children as young as three got up at 5:00 a.m. to work. They would feed the animals, work in the fields or gardens, wash the dishes, practice their knitting . . . not to make little misshapen doilies for Grandma, but to support the family with income revenue. They worked rigorously and completed jobs that were truly helpful to the family's welfare.[6] I'm not talking about rare, abnormally developed, isolated sects of society. This was how much of culture functioned until the most recent period of history. Nothing in the DNA in the human species has changed since then. If the third graders then were capable of keeping cattle alive throughout four seasons, I am pretty sure ours can empty the trash cans without suffering severe mental anguish.

WHAT WORK CAN LOOK
LIKE IN THE HOME

Okay, mamas. This is where the rubber meets the road, and the vacuum meets the carpet. *What does it look like for kids to work in a home?* How much work is good? What are some appropriate jobs? I've shared a few general categories to get you thinking although, of course, every home will look different.

Personal Responsibilities

There are normal daily routines that we do because we're humans living in homes. We brush our teeth, make our beds, bathe or shower, and clean up after ourselves. My guess is your kids are probably doing at least half of these things, so just pat yourself on the back and take a deep, satisfying breath. You're doing a great job, mom! Doesn't that feel nice?

Regular Chores

I like having a rhythm of chores in the family flow. Every day my kids have one or two chores in addition to the daily responsibilities. For example, my nine-year-old may vacuum the downstairs, my seven-year-old may empty all the trash cans, and my toddler might dust the living room. Then Friday is our main chore day where we will do larger projects, like deep clean bathrooms or clean the playroom. At the end everyone gets a treat: the kids enjoy a favorite kids' meal and a show, and Todd and I eat Mexican take-out at our kitchen table. Having a special thing to look forward to at the end of our workday gives us all some needed motivation.

Outdoor Jobs

Recently when my mom was visiting, we sat on the back porch and discussed the issue of kids and work. She looked around the yard with a smile and said, "I promise I could come up with enough jobs around here for your kids to work the entire summer!"

As you look outside, what work do you see that needs to be done? Do you have a fear of walking barefoot lest you squish your feet in dog poop? Do you have weeding, scrubbing, sweeping, plucking, mulching, trimming, or sanding to be done? Whatever you see, your kids can help! Add these to someone's daily jobs, or do them on your family workday. I know that many of us may feel that our schedules, and our kids' schedules, are too busy to include these outside projects. This is to our detriment. If we are too busy to care for our homes and to teach our children how to care for our homes, then we are too busy.

> Every week, every season, should involve caring for our property, beautifying it, and bringing it into order.

I am right here with you on this, mama. Just this week I texted my husband, "I CANNOT HANDLE OUR GARAGE ANY LONGER. We're not showing our kids how to take good care of their stuff." (I know deep down he *loves* when I use all caps in my text messages.) If we have too much to care for, then maybe we have too much. Every week, every season, should involve caring for our property, beautifying it, and bringing it into order.

HOBBIES AS WORK

Most of our hobbies involve some work (except ones like, you know, cheering for our favorite college football team). Whether our kids express interest in baking cookies, fishing, woodworking, sewing, painting, playing guitar, or practicing baseball—it takes planning and preparation to develop a hobby.

As mamas, we can help our kids by encouraging them to (okay, sometimes that looks like *making* them) invest in their hobbies. My sons have a natural gift for golf. There's nothing wrong with saying, "Go outside and hit fifty chip shots in the front yard, and don't come in until you're done!" All hobbies involve some maintenance, in the form of the often-boring work of maintaining our tools or cleaning up after our projects. This is an essential skill that needs to be taught.

THE GIFT OF LEARNING A TRADE

As our kids grow in years, work can look like dabbling in a trade. Recently I chatted with a friend about education. She thought that instead of forcing our kids to be super-whizzes at math and science and *all* the subjects, we should instead direct them to a skill or trade they can use in the real world.

My husband started a lawn-care company when he was a teenager. He mowed lawns for senior adults in the neighborhood who served him lemonade and chatted his ears off. Guess what he spends his days doing now? He works in the landscaping industry and talks to senior citizens about their yards.

Encourage kids to have their little businesses. Let them walk neighborhood dogs, sell homemade bracelets, shadow a car mechanic, interview a nurse or doctor, write mini-novels, dabble in computer programming. It may be surprising how many of these little side jobs have a direct impact on their eventual careers.

More than anything, I feel like our kids need to know that their work matters. My grandmother knew this. If she didn't care for the chickens on her farm, the family wouldn't have eggs to eat. It's harder today to connect the dots, but our kids should feel involved, engaged, and connected to the family cause. Create rituals and routines that involve work, and shower on the praises liberally.

THINGS TO CONSIDER

As you brainstorm your own family traditions, here are some things to consider:

- Do you have positive memories of working as a child? What about negative memories? What made these experiences positive or negative?
- What kinds of chores did you or your husband have as a child?
- What would it look like for your kids to contribute to the family work and to help in ways that would really benefit the family?
- What are some creative hobbies your kids enjoy?

SUGGESTED THINGS TO DO

- Implement a system of responsibilities and chores, such as my friend's Regaining Order in the Home system.[7]
- Write down one actionable step you could make over the next month to get your kids more involved in maintaining the home.
- Assign weekly and daily jobs. Come up with a clear way to display these jobs in your home.
- Evaluate your home and schedule to ensure that your kids have the time, space, supplies, and encouragement to pursue their hobbies.

CHAPTER 11

REST

Sundays Are a Gift, and So Is the Flu

*What is a family? A family is a well-regulated hospital,
a nursing home, a shelter in time of physical need, a
place where a sick person is greeted as a sick human
being and not a machine that has a loose bolt . . . to be
shoved aside because it is no more fun, nor is it useful!*

—EDITH SCHAEFFER[1]

RECENTLY TODD AND I DECIDED TO DO SOMETHING wonderful. We would take our kids to Disney World! There is nothing quite like telling your kids you're taking them to Magic Kingdom. If you could bottle up those few explosively jubilant moments, it would make quite an ointment to apply during the not-so-special parenting experiences, like the time when your son writes "Hi Mom" in black permanent marker on the carpet. (Did you hear me say "permanent marker" and "carpet"?) Anyway, we felt like we were winning at life for our (albeit quick) excursion to "the happiest place on earth." It was all the things. It was special and magical, and there were literal and figurative fireworks for the Smartt family.

But there was one non-magical moment. We were trapped—I mean, waiting—for the Peter Pan's Flight ride in a stuffy, impatient line. I looked down to see my three-year-old rotating her chin and lips on a handrail while plucking at a piece of trash on the ground. In the air was the fragrant aroma of 250+ sweaty and exhausted human beings who had just endured ten hours of amusement park joy. Every once in a while you'd hear a sweet little sneeze or hacking cough from behind you. And I just knew it, deep down in my soul. *We are getting the flu.*

THE GIFT OF LOVING OUR
FAMILIES THROUGH SICKNESS

Two days after we returned home from Disney, I had just finished washing all the laundry and returned the last folded beach towel to its home when my oldest son beckoned to me in that tone of voice that makes every mother's blood run cold for a brief moment. "Mom? My head hurts so bad, and I'm so hot."

I don't know if every mother experiences the same phases of caring for sick kids that I do. In stage one, I am like a tornado. A vicious, immunity-boosting, disinfecting monster. I will defeat this illness. I am frantically sanitizing, obsessively pumping my kids with vitamins and elderberry tonics, slathering anything that moves with essential oils, bustling around the house like a germ-defeating superhero. I laugh in the face of illness!

As you may guess, fairly soon thereafter stage two inevitably sets in, the one in which Mom gets sick. The good news is all moms instinctively know what to do when they're sick. The bad news is we do none of it. We're not hypocrites; we're just servants.

It's hard to rest (what does that even mean as a mom?) when there are still puke buckets to clean and middle-of-the-night feverish calls for water ("with a straw, Mom!"). Meanwhile, there are still, impossibly, people who need food and clean spoons to eat it with. It's inhumane and insufferable.

And then there is stage three, in which you feel life will never again be the same and you will be sick forever. This is the stage where you may brave a field trip to the mailbox, and the whole beautiful outside world will feel overwhelmingly breathtaking. Trees! A neighbor! Fresh air! At this point in the game, any semblance of fighting germs is gone, flushed down the toilet, like the whole box of tissues your toddler used in one morning. You've given up the fight. You're all sleeping in the same bed, sharing the top sheet as a tissue. People are sneezing on the forks as they empty the dishwasher, and it's possible there is throw-up on the hand towel, but you're so tired you don't even care.

As a self-confessed perfectionist and unabashed lover of life's perfect moments, *I hate sickness*. I find it terribly inconvenient to my actual and important life plans. It feels like a pause in the idyllic script I have written for our family.

I have slowly readjusted my perspective on the slow suffering that sick days offer as I realize sick days are ministry. *Good, meaningful work.* Edith Schaeffer says,

> For some people the memory of illness carries with it the memory of loving care, cool hands stroking the forehead, sponge baths in bed, clean sheets under a hot chin, lovely flavored drinks, alcohol back rubs, curtains drawn when fever is hurting the eyes, soft singing of a mother's or father's voice during a sleepless night.[2]

I know she is right. I think back to my own childhood, and while I don't exactly treasure my memories of sick days, I can't deny that they are powerful ones. Being cared for when you are sick has a formative, powerful impact on the growth of an individual. It matters. "When illness hits," Schaeffer continues, "we should remember that this period of time is part of the whole of life. This is not just a non-time to be shoved aside, but a portion of time that counts."[3]

As a child, I had the flu when my parents were out of town, and Aunt Marci drove me to the doctor's office, got me medicine, and settled me cozy into bed. Now that I know how intensely she hates germs, the memory holds even more significance. I remember times when my mom tenderly held back my hair while I gripped a plastic bucket, violently sick to my stomach. Once she baked me chicken nuggets and tater tots, my favorite meal, when after a long illness I was *finally* feeling better. As a mother now, it all makes sense: her concerned eagerness to see me finally eating and drinking again. Later in life my cousin delivered homemade blueberry muffins to my bedside while I was recovering from a traumatic surgery for an ectopic pregnancy. I also recall being tenderly carried to the bathroom by a kind nurse after I was reeling from a difficult childbirth.

The thing is, when a human being is at his weakest and most vulnerable, the time is even more ripe for impact. Sicknesses, injuries, and illnesses offer opportunities we cannot find elsewhere to minister to our families. It is for that reason that I have learned not to scorn these times or roll my eyes and groan inwardly at how our real life is being inconvenienced, but instead, to see these times as unique opportunities—for ministry, for service, and, yes, for memory-making.

Easier said than done, of course. That flu that I mentioned in the beginning of the chapter? While the kids bounced back pretty quickly, for me, the mom, it dragged on for nearly a month. It included bouts with bronchitis, asthma, dehydration, and a sinus infection, rounded out by a nice little stomach bug that came on the back side of it all. It was an awful month that felt like a decade, and I wanted it to be over so badly. The irony is I was knee-deep in the middle of this very chapter when the illness struck. I didn't want to live it; I just wanted to write about it.

> Sicknesses, injuries, and illnesses offer opportunities we cannot find elsewhere to minister to our families.

At the same time I can see the good things it brought in our family, and it gave me plenty of opportunities to implement some of the sickness traditions I preach. Here's the thing: the modern American culture and generation in which I am raising my family like to scorn, disregard, and ignore weakness. But when we finally accept sickness as an inevitable part of life, we can maximize this time instead of wishing it away.

SICKNESS TRADITIONS

It seems odd to have traditions for sickness, doesn't it? But as we've said, these times are ideal for making an impact on our families.

The Gift of Prayer

When you or your family are weak and not able to do much, you can pray. There were many times in this recent sickness when I felt so incredibly behind. Everywhere I laid my eyes there was some unfinished task I did not have the energy to complete. So, what could I do? I could pray. I'm embarrassed to say that it takes a massive respiratory illness to make me finally pause and pray fervently. I used this time to pray for my kids, for God's direction and hand on all my projects, for others in need, for all sorts of things. In a weird way, I miss this time for how it brought me to my knees.

We can teach our children that they can go to their heavenly Father when they're sick and needy. My oldest son has asthma. I cannot count the number of times I have knelt by the side of his bed, holding the nebulizer for his breathing treatment in the dead of night, praying aloud or silently to the God who sees every cell in his body, praying that He would strengthen him and restore him to health. I know my son has heard some of these prayers. What a gift to hear someone praying for you!

I like to view myself and my family as everlastingly energetic and permanently strong. But this is a facade. In sickness, we see ourselves for what we are: thoroughly human and essentially weak. Instead of being depressed at our dismal state, we can lean on the everlasting arms of the Almighty One who never tires, never ages, and never gets weary.

I want to perpetuate this attitude in our home when we're sick. Instead of rushing through sickness, what if we intentionally prayed together as a family, thanking God for the reminder of how big and strong He is and that we can live forever in heaven because of Jesus? It's a mind-set change, and believe me when I say I know God's everlasting strength may be the last thing on your mind when you're rinsing out puke buckets or wiping snotty noses of little people who prefer to remain snotty. But it's a worthy effort to refocus.

Tender Care During Illness

I alluded to this earlier, but perhaps one of the sweetest sick traditions is to tenderly care for those who are sick or injured. Yes, our official plans for the day or week may die, but what is more valuable, really, than being hands and feet of love to someone in a vulnerable state? This gives tremendous import to all those acts that could otherwise seem mundane and monotonous. Bringing a cold drink, with a straw, to feverish lips. Rearranging pillows, getting fresh sheets or a new shirt, changing someone into new pajamas, making a little snack tray of all sorts of yummy choices, putting a cold washcloth on a forehead, wiping someone's face after they throw up, bringing them something interesting to look at, stopping to wipe hair out of eyes and scratch a back—all of these are memories, and powerful ones at that.

This also applies to little boo-boos and injuries. A part of me cringes when I hear a mom or dad say to a little one who's fallen down, "Oh, stop whining. You're fine! It's fine!" Cases of severe dramatics aside (and believe me, I know there are those individuals), most children need and long for a little moment of kindness, attention, and care when they get injured. Maybe they're making it worse than it is. Well, don't all of us do that sometimes? We long for the attention even more than the Advil or the Band-Aid. I try to see their little injuries as opportunities to say, "I notice you. You matter."

The Gift of Slow Days

See the slow pace of sick days as a gift. In health, we are biking, playing, digging, swimming, walking, and/or running the entire day, with little downtime for rest, reflection, or reading. The sick days offer a different rhythm. My kids may reminisce about hearing the *Rush Revere and the Brave Pilgrims* audiobook while cuddled on the couch or about reading *The BFG* in front of the fire when we could hardly hold our heads up from the flu's weakness. And to be fair, no doubt they'll remember episodes of *Little House on the Prairie* streaming from our TV. (Don't get me wrong. There were plenty of mindlessly entertaining television shows the kids watched when I could not muster the strength to read.)

The Forgotten Gift of Slow Recovery

So many have lost the idea of convalescence, and it's a shame. Convalescence is the gradual recovery of health and strength after illness or injury. In our hurry-up-and-feel-better culture, we are wont to skip the convalescence stage. When we face sickness or health setbacks, we want to snap our fingers and recover immediately. Life is not like that, nor are our bodies. We slowly heal. I am a reticent learner, but I am trying to allow my kids and myself the freedom to convalesce and rest. Give yourself time to heal.

The Gift of Remembering Friends During Illness

Our recent illness required me to miss church for a month. I had a few church friends reach out to see if we needed anything, to let me know they were praying, and to let us know we were missed. What kindness! I absolutely cannot tell you how much those texts and e-mails meant. I was embarrassed trying to recall the last time I had reached out to someone because she was sick. Times of infirmity, pain, and setbacks should be tangible reminders of ministry:

- "Guys, wasn't that nice when Grammy brought us home-made soup? Can you help me remember to take food for someone when we are feeling better?"
- "Isn't it awful when you're sick? We should be praying for people who are hurt or sick. Can you think of anyone?"

THE GIFT OF SUNDAYS

I have to admit I have always been confused and a little convicted about how to spend our Sundays. Many Christians pose that we as believers are not required to observe the Sabbath in the officially described Old Testament manner, but it is expedient to observe it as a day of rest.[4] I have settled on the idea that Sunday should look and feel different in our home, with definite times to meditate on God. I want our kids and the world to see that we are different. We may not be *required* to do Sunday a certain way, but I sure have seen blessing when we rest and focus on the Lord.

"Every Sunday, God wants you to be reminded that you are not a machine."[5] I should note I'm saying Sundays, but I don't think the actual day matters much. Many pastors and others work on Sundays, so they observe a Sabbath rest at a different time, for example, from Friday evening to Saturday evening. The point is rest and refocus. "Sabbath is 24 hours of rest and play, a time when we remember that God is in control, that he has lavished our lives with his grace, that he is at work while we are at rest, and that we glorify God through our rest—through 24 hours of being absolutely unproductive."[6]

THE GIFT OF CHURCH

Church is the foundation for Sunday traditions. Growing up, church was a nonnegotiable. Although a few times when the family was exhausted, Dad would declare, "Today, we're visiting Bedside Baptist!" Church didn't feel forced or dreary or mandatory. It was what we did. Weekends are simpler when you establish that church is what you do on Sundays.

When Church Is Hard

I want to add two disclaimers here. One is for the mom of very young children. I can see you reading this, shoulders sagging down, tears rushing to your eyes. The truth is there is a brief (yet everlasting-feeling) stage with a toddler and/or a newborn when church is more exhausting than a marathon. I can't tell you how many times I pulled out of that church parking lot in tears, thinking it had surely been a waste of time and wondering why we bother to go at all.

There was the Sunday my husband was leading worship, and I was cradling a newborn on my shoulder, dragging a screaming toddler by one arm out of the church in the subtlest manner I could manage. (Note: there is no subtle manner to do this.) Then there were the Spilling Years (which we have perhaps emerged from? Please can it be so?). I always felt horrible for whoever made the unfortunate choice to sit behind us and was forced to mop up or pick up: Cheerios, a lunch box and contents, a rubber ball, stickers, lukewarm coffee, orange juice, a bagel with butter, and Matchbox cars. I had always wanted to be that family that came with one single Bible and nothing else, but, alas, I am like a walking Super Target on Sundays. A day of rest? *Ha!* For moms of little ones who choose to attend church, Sunday can seem like the furthest thing from a day of rest. I often thought secretly it was the hardest day of the week, in fact. So why? Why bother to go to church when it is stressful for everyone involved?

Basically because it's not about you.

As I wrote in my e-book, *How to Introduce Your Child to Jesus*:

I have realized I need to change my mindset. As an unmarried, professional, well-manicured, well-rested, way-too-much-free-time adult, church was wonderful. I could arrive with my hot Starbucks, chat with my friends, make eyes with the handsome young single man I had my eye on, sing the hymns undistractedly, listen to the sermon, and actually learn something. *Not so as a mother.* I have made peace with the fact that for the next decade, church is a sacrificial act.

As a mother, most Sundays, instead of a gift I receive, *church is a gift I give*. A gift to the Lord—obeying Him in honoring His day. A gift to my husband and other Christians, in worshipping with them. And to my children, of course. Know this, mama: when you're frustrated from dealing with a loud or cranky little one in church, you are not alone. You are doing the right thing![7]

So that is my first disclaimer, which is essentially a hug I wish I could leap through the pages and give to the exhausted moms for whom church is one long act of obedience. Soldier on, mama! Don't give up the good fight. You are slowly and faithfully creating a beautiful pattern that is a wonderful tradition, perhaps the foundational tradition on which a strong family is built.

> As a mother, most Sundays, instead of a gift I receive, *church is a gift I give.*

And now my second disclaimer. There may be weeks, or seasons, when attending church is not the best option. I would like to take a few moments to sing the praises of a well-done home church. It's not the same, of course, without seeing the faces of other human beings who love Jesus. But timely home church can be a beautiful thing. I was just talking to a friend who has a little baby. We're at the height of a bitter flu season, and she said, "You know, our young church just isn't the best at the sick policy. After months of being sick, we made a family decision to have home church from Christmas through February." In times when someone is homebound, don't think church is an all-or-nothing. I was so tenderly touched by the stories in *The Long Winter* of the Ingalls family honoring the Sabbath in their own homes, though no one else was watching. They'd get their baths, do their hair, put on their Sunday best, do all the work on Saturday, and worship together in their home, even if it meant that no one else ever noticed.[8]

WAYS TO MAKE SUNDAYS SPECIAL

Want to know how to make Sunday special? Start with food, one of my favorite topics. As I view it, there are two different approaches to Sunday meals. We've done both.

Simple Sunday Meal

If people are hungry, mama ain't resting. Unless you plan ahead, that is. When my mom was a child, their family ate cold, no-prep meals all day on Sunday. They'd have bread and butter for breakfast, hard-boiled eggs for lunch, a cold, day-old roast for dinner. Some mamas today exclaim, "It's Sunday! Fend for yourselves!"

My friend Megan invented "Sunday snack dinner," a tradition we've adopted that is both simple and special. The kids love the fun, savory finger foods; we love the relaxed simplicity of paper plate dishes—can I get an *amen*? For a special dessert, we all dive into a box of Trader Joe's snickerdoodles. We light two candles, and Dad reads a chapter from the New Testament as we eat. This has become one of my kids' favorite traditions, and it requires more intention than work.

Elaborate Sunday Dinner

Then there is the classic, beloved Sunday dinner. In the delightful cookbook *A Return to Sunday Dinner*, chef Russell Cronkhite muses:

> Sunday dinner was once an American institution, a strong, familiar thread running deeply through our national fabric. I believe it can be that way again. A return to Sunday dinner can help bring us back to a time of craftsmanship, honor, values and care. It can show us once again that time spent with those we

love—enjoying family games, listening to tales of past struggle and glory, sharing our dreams and disappointments—far outweighs the amusements of the hectic, impersonal world that presses upon us.[9]

Sunday dinner is a ritual I only recently have felt the bandwidth to attempt to accomplish, as we have arrived at that sweet spot of life where all of us are sleeping through the night. I think a Sunday dinner tradition is one of the most beautiful ones you can create. It's a catch-22, because a meal like that definitely requires some effort and work. One way to work around this and still afford the chef a Sabbath rest is to prep a chicken, turkey breast, or pot roast on Saturday and simply pull it out to cook on Sunday. Even many sides can be made ahead: casseroles, mashed potatoes, and veggies to roast. This is where a slow cooker can be your best friend. A slow-cooked pot roast is truly one of the great kitchen miracles. Potatoes and carrots layering the bottom, salted and peppered roast on the top. Frozen rolls, jar of applesauce—BOOM. Amazing dinner.

No matter how you slice it, special Sunday dinner requires a good lump of premeditated work and planning. Yet it's beautifully worth it. The crisp, beautiful tablecloth, the "special" china, a homemade, nourishing, and delicious roast beef dinner with all the fixings—these are the things that people dream of coming home to. A slow, relaxing, treasured Sunday dinner is one of the finest medicines life offers. Whether your kids are teenagers or babies, I assure you that whatever effort you are able to give will be richly appreciated (though maybe not immediately verbalized). You can do it! Make Sunday meals special! Make

> A slow, relaxing, treasured Sunday dinner is one of the finest medicines life offers.

your own tradition, and don't be afraid to change it as life becomes simpler, or for that matter, more complex.

TO REALLY REST, PUT DOWN THAT PHONE

Maybe the most important key to a restful Sunday is to eliminate technology for a designated period of time. And I mean *everything*—answering work e-mails, scrolling social media, and playing games. The whole media shebang (although my husband argues vehemently that professional football games and NASCAR races produce a rather calming background hum and are therefore allowed).

Until we completely disengage from our devices, I think it's hard for us to realize how the steady interruption of beeps and chirps keeps us on mental alert, unable to truly rest. How can we hear from God? How can we enjoy the unfettered downtime with our families when we are constantly attached to our phones? I have had tech-free Sundays for many years now, and I love it so much. I definitely feel myself starting to twitch and crave my phone as I detox from accessing it nonstop. It takes a bit of self-control to wean oneself from the urge to "just check things real quick." But this is good work. The no-tech rest is unlike any other relaxation we could contrive.

THE GIFT OF FAMILY VACATION

I used to secretly wonder if family vacations were excessive or unnecessary. I don't think that anymore. Now, I see that family vacations do things for the family that nothing else can do. In *What Is a Family?*, Edith Schaeffer recalls a family reunion scene that looks a lot like my own family's: cousins throwing a ball with an uncle, father-in-law chatting cordially with daughter-in-law, giddy excitement at exploring a new place, bonding over tasty dessert, morning cups of coffee enjoyed on the back porch.

However, in full disclosure, the Schaeffer family also does a lot of stuff that we don't. Handwritten invitations via mail six months in advance. All the children scribble in vacation journals, recording memories from their day. One of the aunts brings hand-sewn matching outfits for the entire family for their family picture. (Can you imagine?) The kids share their music and art projects from the year. There are games, meandering walks, and deep theological discussions. Oh, she shows the messy parts too—the petty disagreements and overtired toddlers, the heated debates when two people argue through the night, sort it out, untangle hurt feelings—this is a real gathering with real people after all. It struck me reading this account how much work went into this whole thing on every level.

I share this not to make us all feel horrible about how inadequate our own family vacations are but to give us a picture of *what could be* on a family vacation. For many of us, this idyllic vision of a family reunion might make you sad. Maybe you feel it could never happen. Maybe your extended family would never agree to get together for a week, and if they did, it would be an epic disaster. Maybe you're right. But I just want to say two things:

1. There is such a precious gift in sharing a vacation with a big slew of relatives. Maybe it won't ever be the whole family for you, but would you consider inviting your sister, your in-laws, some cousins? Maybe you have some friends who are like family. Who could you start a vacation tradition with?
2. No matter who comes, vacations are messy.

Yes, let's get this point clear out of the gate. Vacations for parents of young children are *not* restful. Same work, different location! And it's not like the kids all get together and say, "You know, Mom and Dad have decided to do something really nice for us. Let's all be on our extra-best behavior." Nope. Instead, you may have one or two who seem to live to make you regret your (expensive) decision. Anytime you're in close quarters, there will be all sorts of ruffled feathers between parents, kids, cousins, in-laws, and every combination thereof.

My parents often take my siblings and me on vacation, and it's bona fide nuts. As I write, there are a total of thirteen kids under the age of nine, five sometimes-hormonal women, and varying personality types (too many cooks in the kitchen). There are rainy indoor afternoons, messy living rooms, and meltdowns over hot dogs sliced the wrong direction or maliciously fired Nerf-gun bullets. Do not get me wrong, we get some beautiful Instagram photos, but I have often thought, *If people could only see what goes on behind the pictures! It's not always idyllic!* Tempers lost, snippy comments, little ones melting down and fighting. Hurt feelings, broken toys, and grumpy moms and dads—the whole gamut.

Yet I literally wouldn't trade these weeks for anything. Truly.

We leave with memories we will have forever. We leave with hours and hours of quality time invested in the people we love most. We leave with a deep assurance that "We are a family." Exhausting? Expensive? Patience-stretching? Yes, yes, yes! Yet infinitely worth it. When you vacation, consider these ways to maximize the memory-making time:

- Have a craft afternoon where everyone creates a special memento to take home.
- Read a book together nightly—your children will always

remember they read that book at the beach (or other vacation spot).

- Consider the power of place and try to visit the same location frequently as a family, whether it's your special rental home or a special lake.
- Give kids a special car-trip binder or bag with fun things to do during the car ride.
- Play the license plate game for longer trips. Pick a certain amount of states, and if you find those states, give yourself a fun reward.
- Listen to a new audiobook in the car to always associate with a particular trip.
- Take the same family picture every trip (the same person covered to the head in sand, all the kids wearing blue, holding hands looking over a mountain, and so forth).
- Collect something to take home: shells, rocks, sticks.

From picture-perfect-but-not-really family vacations, to rich Sunday dinners, to holding puke buckets in the dark—all are memory-making moments! I hope you feel encouraged to create intentional practices of rest in your family.

THINGS TO CONSIDER

As you brainstorm your own family traditions, here are some things to consider:

- Do you recall a time when you were sick or physically in need and someone cared for you?
- Are you satisfied with your weekly rhythm in terms of rest?

What would it look like for you to have a day of rest, in your current stage?

- What family vacations do you treasure from your childhood? What made them special?
- What vacation traditions do you currently have, or could you start one?

SUGGESTED THINGS TO DO

- Put together a "sick bin" of activities, remedies, interesting books, comfortable towels, cleaning supplies, and so on, so that you are ready to love on the members of your family when they are sick.
- Designate at least one section of the week (preferable a whole day) to be tech-free in your home. Find an accountability partner to do it with you.
- List three things you could do differently on Sunday, or another designated day of the week, so that you could rest.
- Choose one vacation tradition you could start or a way you could make an existing vacation more memorable. (See appendix for ideas.)

CHAPTER 12

FAITH

Why You Need the Puzzle Box

Through their years with us, our interaction with
our children will show them who God is and how
He acts. Let's shower them with love and discipline
in the broadest sense and convey as much of God
as they can understand at whatever age they are.

—NOËL PIPER[1]

EVERY SINGLE MORNING, MY HUSBAND ENJOYS THE
same exact routine. He wakes and heads to the kitchen to brew a
cup of coffee: black, with one ice cube. (I know. Non-hot coffee is
nonsense to me too.)

Coffee in hand, he sits down on the gray parlor chair next to
the fireplace. He reaches to the side table for his old, worn black
Bible with his name etched on the front, a groomsman gift. *And
then he reads.* This simple morning routine is a faith tradition, and
it happens like clockwork, early or late, tired or not, busy day or
quiet.

I am not so constant, wavering as I tend to do with a bad night's sleep, disruptive kids, ever-changing schedules in when, or if, I read my Bible. But Todd? He is steady.

As his day goes on, Todd will knowingly and unknowingly engage in a few more rituals. But that moment—the one on the gray chair with the silver buttons down the armrests—that tradition is the anchor that holds the rest in place.

There is a 1000-piece jigsaw puzzle in process on my mom and dad's dining room table at all times. These puzzles are always complex, but some of them are maddening! I never cease to be amazed when I walk in their door and see the latest completed puzzle. I always think, *How in the world? They did it again!*

And how did they do it? Quite simply, they looked at the completed picture on the box. Without the box's guiding image, puzzling would be a frustrating task, a blind attempt to make sense of the jumbled pieces.

Our lives need that puzzle-box picture. We need a guide— clear directions to help us achieve our end goal. *This is what our Christian faith does for us.* It's our puzzle box.

If you read this memory-making book and start a whole slew of new traditions—game night, dates with Dad, pancake breakfast— but you don't understand what God has created you for, then your days, quite frankly, are like that sitting mound of mismatched puzzle pieces: incomplete, lacking framework. Faith makes the rest of our life make sense. It guides everything else.

My husband and I make memories with our kids because we want to introduce them to Jesus. We bake muffins for the neighbors because we want to share God's love with them. I rock my little girl when she's scared at night because I want her to know that she can depend on not only her earthly parents but also her heavenly Father.

I don't arbitrarily choose random traditions just because they seem fun at the time. There is an underlying current, a rubric, that helps us know what's the best use of our memory-making time. Faith is that map, and it tells me where I'm going. Here are the essential truths:

- I was made by a loving God.
- Jesus died the death I deserve so that I can go to heaven forever.
- I will have to answer for the way I have lived my life.
- I want as many people as possible to understand this message too.

This lights a fire under me. Now I have a reason and a purpose for all the other traditions. Making memories is great, but there is a goal larger than capturing that perfect hiking photo, enjoying the best-ever family vacation, or logging years and years of family dinner.

And it's not that these things don't matter as much. To the contrary: what I love about the gospel is that it makes everything else mean more, not less.

It's not just about serving dinner to someone who needs it— it's about bringing hope to another soul who will live forever in eternity. It's not just about laughing together on a family adventure—it's about imparting value to little lives who can literally make ripples in the pond of eternity. Memories simply take on wings and fly when they spread the gospel of Jesus Christ. I hope this perspective helps you choose wisely the celebrations you want for your family.

> What I love about the gospel is that it makes everything else mean more, not less.

So what about faith traditions themselves? How can we celebrate

Jesus specifically in our days and weeks and grow our family in its love for God? Here are a few tools to help you bring faith traditions into your home.

THE GIFT OF MUSIC AND FAITH

Isn't it amazing how vividly one can recall song lyrics? I grew up listening to country music. It is stunning, and a little eerie, that I can hear an old song from Randy Travis or Alan Jackson now and still sing every word. I'm no musical phenom; it's the power of music. So it makes total sense to use music as much as possible with anything we're trying to remember, including things that remind us of our faith.

And we should keep this in mind from the very beginning of a child's life. Whether it is rocking a little baby while you hum a familiar hymn, singing "Jesus Loves Me" with a toddler, or playing Sunday school songs in the car, do not underestimate the power of storing up these songs in your little one's heart. Aunt Jamee wrote and recorded a whole album of Bible songs during our childhood. Even today I can quote you all the words to "Nothing, Nothing, Nothing Can Separate Us!," taken from the memorable passage in Romans. These words have stayed with me for thirty years.

Nearly anything can (and has) been put to music. Anything you want your kids to remember—the Lord's Prayer, the creeds, or catechism questions have been put to song for little ones.[2] We live in such a resource-rich age that we simply have no excuse for not packing our family's minds with rich theology in a winsome way. Play these at mealtimes, in the car, at bedtime. Make them resources that you regularly access.

My kids love listening to new Christian songs from the radio. They have dance parties to their favorite songs in our playroom. I love that. But as much as I do enjoy modern Christian artists, I am a bigger fan of hymns.

Honestly, comparing some of the modern songs to hymns feels a bit like comparing gas station cheese puffs to a gourmet charcuterie platter ornate with farm-fresh cheeses and organic meats. They both feed you, but one is a far richer and more satisfying experience. To carry the analogy a bit further, it does take a bit of developing and honing the appetite. Any kid will eat a cheese puff. Appreciating a high-quality piece of aged cheddar takes a more developed palate. Similarly, we have to work at liking hymns. We have to sit with them awhile, listen once, chew on the words, listen again. Find a better version, play it in the background, over and over, and then! The familiar becomes beloved.

When my husband and I were engaged, we sat in his apartment with two musical friends, trying to pick a song to be played during our wedding ceremony. Suddenly I heard the lyrics of an old hymn redone: "The Love of Christ Is Rich and Free." My husband and I locked eyes; the deal was sealed when we heard the second verse:

> His loving heart engaged to be
> Their everlasting Surety
> 'Twas love that took their cause in hand
> And love maintains it to the end.[3]

First of all, it had the word *engaged* in it, so that was basically a sign because so were we! More significantly, I knew intrinsically, even as a blushing, naive twenty-six-year-old bride, that we were entering into new, precarious ground in this marriage thing, and we needed Someone stronger than us to hold us together. Sometimes we'll sing this song in church, and what a deep, deep assurance these familiar words are to us, a beautiful reminder that God "took our cause in hand." He has led us through three kids, ten years, and innumerable trials, and His "love will maintain it till the end."

When we sing faith songs that have existed for hundreds and hundreds of years and across continents and language barriers, we, too, are acknowledging there is something beyond ourselves. We are admitting connection, linking arms with humanity, and uniting together despite our many differences.

THE GIFT OF MEMORY

Kids memorize things so very quickly—often more quickly than we do. Simply repeat the same thing for a month, and you will be shocked at how much of it they will recall. My childhood church often said the Apostles' Creed and the Nicene Creed; I can quote them verbatim to this day. Whether we encourage our kids to memorize Bible verses, chapters, or some of the ancient creeds or catechism questions, I believe that these ten minutes or less can be the most valuable time you could spend.

Of course, our prayers and worship should be real and not merely repeated mindlessly. But when we memorize prayers, creeds, and hymns, and when we recite these regularly, there is a deep, profound gift being imparted to us on a level that we do not totally understand at the time.

"Morning time," says Cindy Rollins of her homeschool routine, "was a liturgy that offered my children tethers from the past with which they could carry far into the future, to places I am unable to even imagine."[4]

When my kids were very little, my friend Aleece gave me some ABC Bible verse cards that she'd laminated and hooked together. My kids were toddlers, so it was a perfect way to begin memorizing. My sweet little two-year-old son had his favorite. He was a quiet little soul, but when you asked him to say the F verse, his chest would puff up with pride and he would say it loudly. "For God did not give us a spirit of *timinitidy*," he'd say, "but of power [he'd flex his biceps], and of *wuv*, and self-*discipwine*." It was the most precious thing. If we hear this verse, we all look at him now and smile. It's his special verse, and I hope that God uses these words in a mighty way in his life.

Here are some ideas to get your family regularly memorizing Scripture:

- Choose a few verses or passages you'd like to memorize each year and pick a time to say them: in the car, at a meal, upon waking, and so on.
- Consider offering a reward when your children reach a Scripture memory goal.
- Perhaps they could memorize something for a Christmas gift to a grandparent. One Christmas my boys memorized John 1:1–11 for my dad's present, and he loved it.

THE GIFT OF PRAYER

When I am lying in bed trying to fall asleep, I often recall this quote and pray for each of my children: "What an encouragement it is for a child to know that his parents and siblings are praying for him! Each child needs us to pray for him or her every day."[5]

And then, of course, we also have the honor of teaching our kids how to pray on their own. My husband usually prays with our boys when he puts them to bed. When they were toddlers, they'd all kneel beside the bed and Todd had them repeat after him: "Thank you for Mommy." *Thank you for Mommy.* "Help me to have a good attitude." *Help me to have a good attitude.* And so on.

Todd is showing them that he prays, teaching them how to pray, and making it a positive experience. It is not long, and that's okay. Then later, we have them pray on their own.

What if your child doesn't want to pray? The best advice I've heard is don't make him pray. Just say, "That's fine; you can pray to God in your head. I'm going to pray out loud, and you can pray with me." If you aren't in the habit of regular prayer times, mealtime prayers are a wonderful place to begin. There are some beautiful mealtime prayers rich with meaning. You can make an Internet search and find several that could be a good starting place.

THE GIFT OF FAMILY DEVOTIONS

If we want our kids to know God's Word, the solution is simple: family devotions.[6] There are a million pictures of the way this could look. You could sing hymns, ask and answer catechism questions, say the Lord's Prayer, or read from the Bible, a children's Bible, or a devotional book. Sometimes Mom or Dad pray; sometimes everyone prays. The important thing is to make the practice consistent. "We don't forget to eat, and we feel icky if we don't remember to brush our teeth. How wonderful it is when family worship is just as normal a part of the day—so the day is uncomfortable and off-kilter without it."[7]

I even know families who do an all-out church service together each night, and this is very impressive: hymn singing, catechism recitations, devotions, Scripture, prayer. But I say, if devotions aren't something you have been consistent with, start simple. Just add one book to your evening, such as a devotional or children's Bible.

Maybe a daily routine seems like too much. I was just chatting with a friend the other day who said, "We can't make devotions happen each night, but we always have a family devotion on Sunday nights. It's better than nothing." Absolutely! Better a small, consistent routine than no routine or one you simply stop after a week.

Why is this so hard for us to implement? The simple answer is that we are too busy. "Something is wrong if a person, even a pastor and his wife, have so many meetings to attend that the family, the children, can never have time for questions or the togetherness which brings natural questions and answers," Edith Schaeffer notes.[8] Shaeffer goes on to suggest that parents should become comfortable with saying something like, "I'm sorry, Bill, but I can't join you tonight. This is our special time to spend reading God's Word with our kids." I don't know about you, but that reply is one that I need to get in a better habit of repeating!

THE GIFT OF CONVERSATION

The way we talk about things shows how we feel about them. If you want your children to have a tradition of love, respect, and reverence for God, then it's important to watch how you talk about Him. For instance, instead of taking His name in vain or allowing jokes that make light of God and spiritual things, adopt a reverent tone. We should be inspiring awe and wonder, not irreverence or unhealthy fear.

In everyday conversations, marvel at how wonderful God is. Here are a few examples for young children:

- "Who do you think made this wonderful snow?"
- "Isn't God amazing that He made men to know how to build those skyscrapers?"
- "Let's pray together that we can find your watch. God knows everything! He can help."

- "Aren't you glad that God made us all better from our sickness? Be sure to tell Him thank you in your heart."

The nature and spirit of conversations with our kids during every stage of their lives should point back to God as the Creator and Orchestrator of life with the appropriate amount of reverence. This is even more relevant as kids approach the age of sarcasm and skepticism! Find ways to bring God into your everyday talk, acknowledging His goodness in everything you see.

As kids grow and become more curious, they will develop genuine questions about faith. You won't have all of the answers, so when you don't know, ask them to engage with you in researching, reading, and figuring it out together.

This past year we have experienced several deaths in different circles close to us: an uncle, a friend's baby girl, a cousin's sister-in-law. My little niece has been observing and absorbing, and my sister said she suddenly had many questions about death, heaven, and hell. My sister felt somewhat ill prepared to answer many of these questions on the spot, but she tried. "Children's questions," says Edith Schaeffer, "must be taken seriously at the ages of two and three, or they won't be continuing to ask you at twelve and twenty-three."[9] Most likely these questions won't pop up when you have planned for it. We should have a spirit ready to take these questions seriously, despite the plans of the day, our exhaustion, or the imperfect time they're asked. I'm reminded of the Bible verse, "Preach the word; be prepared in season and out of season; correct, rebuke and encourage—with great patience and careful instruction."[10]

We may not always feel ready to discuss life's serious issues. Somehow these opportunities to talk about faith always seem to come when I'm scrubbing a toilet or feel too exhausted to have a bedside chat. But we must see these rare opportunities for the gems that they are. We don't know when a little one's curiosity will be piqued again or what hard questions or anxieties an older child may be grappling with. We must do our best to use every opportunity wisely because we don't know how many more may come.

THE GIFT OF LOVE

The final faith tradition that honestly may perhaps make the most difference in your home is the gift of love. There's no point in doing all of the right things if you don't also create an atmosphere of forgiveness, faithfulness, kindness, and dependability. My siblings and I are in our thirties, and even still, there is nowhere else we'd rather be than our parents' house. We are loved there, it's fun, and it's still home to us.

Edith Schaeffer describes the loving parent so well: "And when the little one patiently climbs the stairs, dragging a toy behind him or her, seeking you, *really seeking you*, wanting communication of some sort—what is the reception? What kind of example are you of God's promise that 'Him that cometh to me I will in no wise cast out'?"[11]

One thing I absolutely love about my sister-in-law Julianne is that she is everlastingly friendly and cheerful to all. Since my children have been very little, she has always given them her fullest attention. They'd wander over to her, and she'd pull them onto her lap, put her arm around them, ask them intently about their favorite new activity or toy. I've always noted this and try to offer the little ones in my life my friendship and willingness to be present, now, with them.

THE SECRET TO IT ALL (YES, REALLY)

So there it all is. The whole list of things we should do and long to do in our homes. And when we fail or falter, let's not give up but get up and try again. Wherever we may be in our faith journeys, whatever we've gotten wrong or fallen behind in, today is the day we can make new traditions (or restart those old ones we've lost). We can begin exactly where we are, with our weaknesses and doubts and inconsistencies. Our loving Father longs to help us point our families to Him.

And lest you think it goes perfectly in my house, goodness no! Lately I'd feared we hadn't taught our third child as many Bible stories as we had our older kids (typical youngest child problems). One Sunday I asked her to review what her Bible story had been in children's church that morning. I'd cheated—the coloring page was Daniel in the lions' den. *This should be a home run,* I thought. She's certainly heard it before, and it has a gratefully simple story line. She can get this one. I smiled as she opened her mouth wide to answer.

"My story," she began with a giant smile, "was about a tiger! And God saved that tiger! He did! And if you pray to bad guys, they will come get you!"

Todd and I looked at each other with wide eyes and burst into laughter. Well, she certainly nailed that one! If you're familiar with the story of Daniel and the lions' den, you know that's not quite the story line. We can laugh at this, but the hard truth is this story is marrow-deep with significance for me. I try so badly to do the faith thing right. I want more than anything to pass down my faith to my kids. And yet it never quite goes how I think it will. And it's hard. It takes a lot of repeating, correcting, trying again, reminding. And at nearly every corner, it's the reminder that we all, every last one of us, are profoundly human, misguided, imperfect, and in need of Jesus' grace to meet our hearts and draw us to Him. Our whole family needs Jesus. We will never do it perfectly. We can try to cram the facts and stories and lessons into their brains, but we just need Him.

And this is why I end with a call to pray and to rest in God's grace for our families. Is there anything more powerful? What a terrific comfort to know that while we fall short as parents, Christ will never fail them. Isn't that the whole point of this Christianity thing after all? That what we could not do, Christ did? May we parent with deep conviction to steward their little hearts well, but may we know even more deeply that it is God who holds them in the palm of His hand.

> What a terrific comfort to know that while we fall short as parents, Christ will never fail them.

THINGS TO CONSIDER

As you brainstorm your own family traditions, here are some things to consider:

- What, if anything, do you remember from your childhood that helped you to have a meaningful faith in the Lord?
- What are your favorite faith-centered books, verses, or songs?
- How could you use music or memory to inspire your kids' faith?
- How could you add or improve on your current family devotional routine?

SUGGESTED THINGS TO DO

- Read a chapter in the book of John together as a family one night a week at dinner.

- Buy a children's Bible or devotional book and read it together before bedtime.
- Pray for your children each night.
- Have a morning or afternoon Bible devotional time together. Everyone reads their own book. Let the kids see you reading. Give them their own Bibles, pens, journal, and "cup of coffee" (juice or water in a fancy-looking cup does the job). It doesn't need to be a long thing (and it probably won't be!), but your kids will notice your example and begin to form devotional habits of their own.
- Enjoy good music. Find a hymn you like in a version you enjoy and play it regularly. You could also choose one hymn or praise song for each child—it could become a "my song" for each child.
- Consider giving each child a life verse. You can frame it for his or her bedroom—birthday gift idea!

QUESTIONS YOU
MAY BE ASKING

What suggestions do you have for families where one spouse is on military deployment or has a demanding travel situation? How can you continue celebrating through distance and change?

My mother-in-law has some wonderful advice for this. My father-in-law was a captain in the navy and spent long periods of time serving overseas during the Persian Gulf War. Her advice is to continue your traditions as much as you possibly can. But sometimes you need a little extra fun. For example, one Christmas when the three kids were in elementary school, my father-in-law wasn't going to be home. Instead of sitting around being sad, my mother-in-law packed everyone up and took the Palm Springs tramway up a mountain where they could actually see snow. I love her joy and determination to add sparkle to life instead of throwing a pity party. As a side note, every one of her children has inherited this make-the-best-of-it spirit, and what a gift that is. Another military wife said that she takes her son out for dinner the day her husband deploys. This is another way of choosing to set an example of joy for our kids even when we are feeling sadness and loss.

QUESTIONS YOU MAY BE ASKING

What suggestions do you have for divorced or single parents as they create traditions?

For families who have experienced divorce, loss, or brokenness, times of celebrating the big holidays and milestones can be tense and difficult. While there's no way I can fully do this subject justice here, I do want to acknowledge that certain traditions can be more difficult for some families than for others. All memory-making mamas will face unique challenges, and this is one of them.

I want to share two things specifically for divorced parents, though. First, the custodial spouse can look for traditions that help the kids stay connected to the noncustodial spouse when appropriate. This is certainly not easy and will look different for each family, but that connection can be a tremendous gift to the children— whether in a lasting, loving relationship or valued memory.

Second, keeping family traditions as life continues without one parent present is important. But feel freedom to joyfully break them when family spirits are down. My neighbor Jennifer hastily packed the car, throwing in blankets and bags with a flourish, on her first Christmas alone with her three daughters. "We're going to the beach for the day," she said resolutely. "It's a three-hour drive, but we need to do this. We need to see the beach." What a joyous way to break the disappointment with courage and spark, and what a wonderful example to her watching daughters.

What suggestions do you have for families who have lost someone and are grieving?

Experiencing a tradition for the first time after you've lost someone can be incredibly difficult. At the same time it's important that grown-ups understand how cathartic traditions can be for children who are grieving. Traditions are a tool to help people through the healing process. For children, the most difficult thing is to not have continuity. Otherwise, they feel that they have not only lost a parent but also lost special celebrations and dependable routines. So even though it feels difficult, enabling them to still celebrate certain traditions can help them heal.

Several years ago speaker and blogger Brittany Price Brooker lost her husband suddenly and was faced with the incredible responsibility of being a single parent to three very young boys. Her advice: "Make traditions about being present with each other and not perfect. 'Perfect' can create stress, but focusing on being present creates sweet memories, fun, and laughter. I also would say it's OK to keep some of the old memories you had; just because it's a new family doesn't mean that you have to get rid of a precious tradition the kids enjoyed before. God will show you how to navigate and seek Him on how to do it for each of the precious and hurting hearts in your home. After death it may take a couple of years to have strength to do a tradition that same way, and that's okay. If you need time, give it to yourself."[1] Such wise, experienced words from a young mama who traveled this difficult road.

My Aunt Jamee, a grief facilitator for children, says, "I can't emphasize how important it is to continue a tradition that a child loves. Grief recovery and healing is all about how to function and still connect when the person isn't there personally. The tradition is a bridge for that." It can be a big thing, like a weekend fishing trip with an uncle instead of Dad, or a small thing, like hanging an ornament that reminds them of Grandma. Some people still celebrate a loved one's birthday with a visit to the graveyard, balloons released, a visit to a favorite spot. For example, her family honors their beloved Pop-Pop with an annual golf tournament. Held near to the weekend anniversary of his death, all of his family come together as they remember the one who loved golf and introduced them all to it. It's a nonmorbid, enjoyable way of honoring his life.

Along this line, you can honor a person by baking recipes that that person enjoyed or visiting a favorite spot of theirs.

I'm on a very tight budget but I want to make memories with my family. What specific tips do you have for me to make memories?

I asked my friend Erin Odom, author of *More Than Just Making It* and *You Can Stay Home with Your Kids*, for her advice on this topic. She suggested many free or cheap memory-making opportunities, such as biking, picnics, movie night at home, library trips, local parks, restaurants with Kids Eat Free nights, and hikes. I also know from experience how difficult it is to attempt to make a budget balance when it just won't work. I know the feeling of having to make cuts and then make more cuts. Even still, I would suggest that memory-making be considered a line item worth fighting for. Even if you can retain only one small, precious tradition (like ice cream cones on the first day of summer, or the apple-picking tradition that everyone just loves), I would advise battling to keep it. It may require some adjustments (for example, maybe we only go out for dessert, not dinner; or maybe we go to the beach for just one night, not a week—you get the point). But I would say, fight for your memories. Scrimp, pinch, and save to keep a few old ones, and then devise new traditions that are free or cheap. *Often, it is in times of financial stress that these little anchors in our families are needed most.*

I still recall vividly a scene in the book *Ramona and Her Father*, which I read years ago. The Quimby family is facing the awful scenario of Mr. Quimby losing his job. The effects are felt by everyone, even eight-year-old Ramona. There is the most precious chapter near the end of the book that I have carried with me all these years into adulthood. Smack-dab in the midst of the financial stress, Mr. Quimby says one evening, "Let's all go get hamburgers!"

The girls can't believe it. They savor every single delicious cheesy, ketchup-filled bite of goodness. Nothing changed in their circumstances, but it seemed to say to the children, "Things are going to be okay."

What suggestions do you have for families who want to incorporate traditions of another culture, whether they've adopted from another culture, or one side of the family is from another culture, and so on?

One wonderful way to open your family's world is by reading. I recommend the book *Give Your Child the World* by Jamie Martin for a comprehensive list of cultural stories. My friend who has adopted interracially says, "One thing that adoption has taught me is the benefit of stepping out of my own circle and exposing my kids to other cultures' traditions. Last year I went to an African Drumming class at the library, and while my initial thought was to engage in the class because of my adopted son, I realized after watching our other children participate and learn about African dance and storytelling what a benefit it was for them to be able to learn from another culture as well. I have to educate myself to make sure I'm not engaging in something that would be inappropriate, but I definitely welcome opportunities to learn from and appreciate other traditions and cultures with my kids. It takes intentional work and time as a parent to dig in and really educate yourself. Humble yourself and do the work to learn from people who reflect the heritage you want to honor."

When do you know that a tradition needs to die?

Oh, what a sad thought for the memory-making mom! Yet it's a part of the whole thing, isn't it? As I write this book, my kids are still fairly little. I know that one day they won't be jubilant about a trip to the zoo. One day they may not race to the car for our annual Christmas-lights viewing session. It is a little sad but a precious warning to treasure these childhood milestones while we have the time.

Our children *will* grow up. It takes wisdom to discern when to let a tradition go. We should hold our traditions but hold them loosely. Traditions are not a tyrant. We have all, perhaps, attended some event where the planner was so intent on things being perfect that it wasn't any fun. Maybe some of us have even been that planner. (Ahem.) Traditions are a wonderful tool to love our families and remind us what matters. But if it's not loving our families and no one is appreciating the reminder, then it's time for a change.

The key here is not to quit Christmas and throw up our hands in despair but to embrace the new gift we've been given and make a new tradition. This will be the case whether we have emerging teenagers who aren't into decorating Christmas cookies on Christmas Eve anymore or whether we have married off children to begin their own families. There should be an openhandedness to our celebrating and a willingness to embrace a new tradition. In every tradition that dies, there is a chance for a new one to grow. And maybe for an old one to be tweaked and to grow up with your family. For example, maybe no one wants to get in their pajamas for a Christmas-lights drive, but adding a Starbucks stop might make this nostalgic tradition still enjoyable.

My parents realized that, as we all have kids and spouses, our family Christmas would never be *on* Christmas Day. So we have started a new tradition: we all spend the night (all twenty-three of us, including thirteen kids) at my parents' home on New Year's Eve, and we have appetizers, gifts, stockings, a huge breakfast buffet, a DIY-gift exchange—the whole Christmas shebang, just a week later. The reality is that my parents are sometimes alone on Christmas morning, but they've chosen to joyfully anticipate our new ritual together.

What do you do when Mom or Dad is in a rough spot and struggling to muster up the gumption to keep doing a tradition? How do you know if it's okay to cancel a tradition temporarily?

There will definitely be times where pulling out all the stops for a celebration is a particular challenge. It's a valid question. In a season of illness, fatigue, grief, anxiety, or depression, are we to "soldier on" inexorably? Should we feel guilty if we quit? The first good step is to ask yourself, "What is this tradition *really* about?" It's not really about the certain mountain house we always go to in fall, for example. It's about us being together. So is there another way we can make that happen?

One year we ate Easter dinner at a restaurant because my mom had been very sick. It wasn't the traditional homemade rolls and ham, but did it matter? Not a bit! If you're feeling very overwhelmed at a particular tradition, ask yourself: "If we don't do *this* tradition, what could we do instead that we all would love?"

I have very small kids. I love all these ideas, but it seems really over-whelming. Do you have tips for me?

First of all, trust me when I said that I was not doing all this stuff when I had babies. We went many years without really having any special family traditions, so if you're already thinking of this topic, you're ahead of the game. Start small, but start somewhere. Pick very small number of traditions that are super easy. Choose one tradition to try in each of the major categories that are important to you: One faith tradition, such as saying the Lord's Prayer before bed. One birthday tradition, even if it's as simple as a giant balloon at dinner. And maybe one good tradition for each season. Then try to be faithful to do them. As time allows, you can add more.

I had a horrible childhood. My family never had traditions. Do you have any encouragement?

You may not be able to eliminate the sad feelings that accompany the holidays, but it can be really powerful to look outward. *Instead of focusing on the things that are not, think about the people in your life you do have, who also need traditions.* Think of your children. How can you love them by celebrating what matters most? Look around. Are there other families, elderly people, neighbors, singles who may also feel lonely during Christmas? You can rewrite the story, remember? You can be the one to start a rich home, and you can be the one who gives life and warmth to many, many people!

I don't have good community around me, so a lot of these ideas seem as though they wouldn't work for us.

I am really encouraged by Sally Clarkson when I think about this topic. Sally and her husband, Clay, often struggled with loneliness during holidays. They chose to do two things: make their own nuclear family rich with traditions and invite lonely people into their home. They made community wherever they were, even when it felt like a randomly gathered, ragamuffin group.

I want to have traditions, but I struggle to make things happen. What do I do if I'm not a planner type?

My first suggestion would be to look in your own family and see if there *are* any planner types, whether it be your husband or an older child to whom you could delegate the responsibility of being in charge of the tradition *countdown*. My second suggestion would be to capitalize on your strengths. Maybe you're not consistent but you have lots of fabulously fun ideas. Be intentional to follow through on a few ideas each year that strike you. For example, you may not always have the same exact Christmas craft time, but it can become a tradition in itself that every season you have a day to do some type of fun activity. See the appendix to select a few traditions you feel really passionate about, and then set reminders on your phone to implement them in the right season.

I usually do most of the planning, and my husband doesn't seem to appreciate what I'm doing. How can I encourage him to be involved?

Well, that can be a common thing in marriage, can't it? We are often wildly different from and even misunderstood by our husbands. I would really try to make traditions that the *unexcited* husband would like, and make sure they're not all things only you enjoy. What things does he really love, and how could those be incorporated into traditions? I would elicit a lot of feedback on what things he values.

If you still have a grumpy spouse, I would try not to focus too much on how your actions are received but continue to give gifts of memory-making to your family. It's probable your children and husband appreciate your efforts, or will in the long run, anyway.

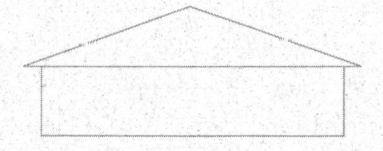

ACKNOWLEDGMENTS

TO MY HEAVENLY FATHER, EVERYTHING I HAVE COMES from You. May You use this work for Your kingdom.

Todd, this book would not be without you. You've given me space to create and picked me up when I doubted myself.

Sam, Ty, and Ellie, I love being your mommy. You're my favorite people to make memories with.

Mom and Dad, you gave us the best family. We were loved well, and now we can love well. Mom, this book is laced with your wisdom. If I'm half the mom you are, mission accomplished. Dad, you believed in me way before I believed in myself. No one has ever been a bigger cheerleader for his children than you are for us.

Julie, you aren't just a best friend; you're a trusted adviser. All my harebrained ideas are better after you are finished with them.

Jenny, my most faithful reader and best friend, my children and yours are blessed by your sacrificial love.

John, there never was a more generous or fiercely loyal little brother. I'm so proud of the man you've become.

Morgan, Helen, and Julianne, my bonus sisters, each of you is so dear to me. I hope I can be half the friend to you that each of you has been to me.

Carole and Doug, you've loved me as your own daughter. Thanks for making memories with my kids.

Ashley, Catherine, and Emily, you've been cheerleaders and prayer warriors when I needed it most.

Bill Jensen, the best agent, thank you for entrusting me with this idea. I hope I've made you proud. I am thankful for your fatherly wisdom and unmatched publishing intuition.

Debbie Wickwire, thank you for remaining gracious while fielding my 957 questions (a day), for getting all my jokes, and for being smart as a whip. You are a joy to work with.

Daisy Hutton, you championed this idea from the beginning and remained a gem throughout.

Thanks to Paula Major, Kate Etue, Denise George, Ashley Reed, Kristi Smith, Becky Melvin, and the entire W Publishing Group team for your wholehearted partnership and incredible ideas! This project is infinitely better because of your fantastic insights and hard work.

Erin Odom, your generous heart and "connecting skills" made my dream possible, and I'm grateful to you.

My Christian Author Mastermind sisters, Grace-Filled Bloggers, and Hope*Writers: I guess it's possible to write a book without friends like you, but I'm just not sure how.

And thank you, finally, to all the friends who generously offered their insights, traditions, and visions for this project: Sheila Carlberg, Morgan Hawk, Rebecca Wetzel, Brittany Price Brooker, Katie Clark, Amy Frank, Jamie Martin, Carole Smartt, John Haggan, Dan Chittock, Jenny Haggan, Julie Chittock, Cyndee Hawk, Jamee Wetzel, Molly, Kelly Tarasovitch, Jeff and Lauren Pyles, and Jenn Fromke.

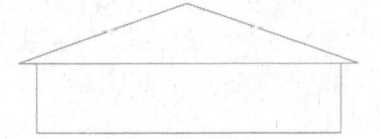

APPENDIX

200+ Great Memory-Making Ideas

BEAUTY TRADITIONS

1. Serve a beautiful family dinner with flowers and linens for special occasions and even have the kids dress in clean clothes.
2. The week of Christmas have a candlelit Christmas dinner with fine linens and fancier foods.
3. Invest in a few beautiful seasonal decorations, buying them off-season for a deal.
4. Gift your kids with a beautiful journal or Bible for their quiet times.
5. Allow each child a small plot in the garden or a special pot where he or she can plant and care for something of his or her own choice.
6. Save rocks from family hikes or trips to parks and write the name and date on them.
7. Purchase sketchbooks for your kids; take nature walks and sketch something you see.

8. Appreciate good music together. Consider introducing your kids to some amazing classical pieces, such as "Simple Gifts" from *Appalachian Spring* by Aaron Copland, "The Lark Ascending" by Ralph Vaughan Williams, and "Canon in D" by Johann Pachelbel.

FALL TRADITIONS

1. Have a family pumpkin carving contest.
2. Go apple or pumpkin picking.
3. Drive through the mountains to look at the leaves.
4. Make a fall bucket list that includes the things you love, such as a mountain hike, apple and pumpkin picking, hayride, corn maze, and river fishing.
5. Host a fall-themed neighborhood block party, like a chili cook-off.
6. Make your own apple cider or apple pie.
7. Read poems about fall.
8. Make your own leaf rubbings.

WINTER TRADITIONS

1. Make chicken soup, shepherd's pie, or hot cocoa on the first snowfall.
2. Make or fill a bird feeder for your outdoor friends.
3. Have a cozy movie night on a freezing evening.
4. Read a book aloud by the fire.
5. Work at a soup kitchen together.
6. Have an indoor campout.

SPRING TRADITIONS

1. Grow a family garden.
2. Provide each child with a personal flowerpot where he or she can grow his or her own fruit or flower.
3. If you have little kids, do Easter egg hunts over and over in the house and yard. They love it even if there's nothing in the eggs!
4. Pull chairs up to a window and watch a thunderstorm together.

SUMMER TRADITIONS

1. Celebrate National Donut Day on the first Friday in June.
2. Visit a hot air balloon festival.
3. Go tech-free for one week. (You may be surprised how much you all enjoy this one.)
4. Celebrate National Ice Cream Day on the third Sunday in July with homemade ice cream or a trip to a local shop.
5. Have a low-country boil and eat outdoors. (This summer one-pot meal of shrimp, sausage, corn, and potatoes is famous in the low country of Georgia and South Carolina.)

FOOD TRADITIONS

1. Have a Saturday special breakfast, whether it's donuts from a local shop or homemade pancakes.
2. Serve pancakes in the shape of whatever holiday it is.
3. Have a family Valentine's fancy dinner the week of Valentine's Day.

4. If you have a husband or loved one who travels a lot, make dinner the theme of wherever they are traveling.
5. If you're studying a certain area in school, eat the foods of that culture.
6. Make sugar cookies for each holiday.
7. Have a kids-takeover night where the kids plan and cook the food and clean up.
8. Let your little ones cook with you, giving them random things to mix up. (As long as you know they won't eat it!)
9. Let the birthday child pick the meal.
10. Make cinnamon bread for special holidays, in a special shape (bunny, wreath, heart, and so on), and for birthdays in the shape of the number for the age your child is becoming.[1]
11. Make a big deal out of certain meals that one person makes really well. "Dad's famous chicken" or "Mom's spaghetti."
12. Sunday snack dinner! Make it easy on Mom. Serve snack foods, such as cheese, bread, fruit, nuts, and vegetables.
13. Have one *easy* night each week for the kids (pizza or chicken nuggets, for example); then the parents can have a special dinner later.
14. Celebrate Pi Day (3.14) with homemade pie.
15. Create a traditional Christmas and Easter breakfast.
16. At least once in the summer, celebrate with an ice cream party after bedtime.
17. Play "restaurant" when you need to use up leftover food.
18. Choose one day a week to make a special treat or dessert, like homemade cookies, bread, or a favorite dessert with dinner.
19. Have a special Christmas tea party.
20. Make "bread in a bag." Lots of recipes for this are available online. It's a simple way for kids to prepare their own individual loaves of bread.

21. Make "coffee mug" brownies. This is a cute and very adaptable recipe for an individual dessert.
22. Have a pizza night and let each person make their own individual pizza.
23. Have fondue night. Prep the materials together and enjoy dipping and tasting.

CHRISTMAS

1. Do an act of service every day in Advent.
2. Create an Advent bucket list and schedule one Christmas activity every day.
3. Give books to your kids and husband for Christmas.
4. Advent wreath making: using clippings from a tree farm, form a wreath and add five candles that you light throughout each week of Advent.
5. Light the candles and have a fancy dinner on Sundays during Advent.
6. The Jesse tree: you can order this online or make your own. Each night you hang ornaments to do with Jesus—His ministry, birth, prophecies about Him, His names—on a little Christmas tree.
7. Wrap your Christmas-themed picture books, then unwrap and read one each day in Advent.
8. Host a neighborhood Christmas-carol sing and serve cookies and hot chocolate.
9. Go Christmas caroling. We have done it the last few years and people love this lost art.
10. Take Christmas cookies to Dad or Mom's office.
11. Have a gingerbread man or gingerbread house decorating contest.

12. Instead of a white-elephant gift exchange, where family members bring small gifts to exchange randomly, have everyone bring a gift they have made. My family does this, and it is always wonderful to see everyone's creations.

13. Instead of, or in addition to, writing a letter to Santa, write a letter to Jesus on His birthday.

14. The day you put up your tree, sleep under it.

15. Give your kids a Christmas ornament that represents something meaningful from the year so they will have a collection to begin decorating their own trees someday.

NEW YEAR'S EVE (AND NEW YEAR'S DAY)

1. Make a list of the answered prayers of your family from the past year.

2. With your older children especially, share the highs and lows of your year and what God has taught you.

3. Have a game night, movie marathon, or dance party with the kids on New Year's Eve. For older children, you could organize a cooking challenge or contest for the meal. For example, everyone could make an appetizer and have judges vote on a favorite.

4. Cook Beans and Greens on New Year's Day.

5. Make some family goals for the year or a family bucket list.

VALENTINE'S DAY

1. Make cookies with gobs of icing and deliver to Dad at his office.

2. Look for stickers, doilies, hearts, stamps, and ribbons on sale

all year long and save them up. Then drag it all out and make a Valentine's Day *mess* while making cards for everyone you know and love.

3. Give your daughters flowers.
4. Consider having a fancy dinner with your whole family on Valentine's Day, and then go out on another, less-crowded night that week with your husband.
5. Make your little ones a handmade valentine, even a simple construction-paper heart.

SAINT PATRICK'S DAY

1. Saint Patrick was an amazing man, so pick up a good storybook and read with your kids about his life. I recommend *The Story of St. Patrick: More Than Shamrocks and Leprechauns* by Voice of the Martyrs.
2. Cook an Irish meal, such as corned beef and cabbage, beef stew, or shepherd's pie, served with Irish soda bread.

EASTER

1. In January, put the start of Lent on the calendar.
2. Use *The Jesus Storybook Bible* to read through the Bible during Lent.
3. Read biblical fiction, based on the Easter story, together at bedtime. Two of our favorites are *Jotham's Journey* and *Amon's Adventure* by Arnold Ytreeide.
4. Build a resurrection garden.
5. Recreate the Passover Seder meal and Jesus' washing of the disciples' feet.

6. During Holy Week, have kids use Play-Doh and craft pipe cleaners to create scenes of the week surrounding Jesus' death.[2]
7. Watch *The Greatest Story Ever Told* or *The Passion of the Christ* with older kids, or share the *Jesus* film with friends.
8. Practice giving up something for Lent as a family.
9. Use Resurrection Eggs with your kids.
10. For a fun twist on an Easter egg hunt, inside the eggs place papers with activities. For instance, it may be a coupon to do a fun thing later or even an exercise or game (Donuts with Dad! or Do ten jumping jacks!).
11. Consider downloading a devotional app for Lent to go through as a family.
12. Participate in a family media fast during Holy Week or all of Lent.

MOTHER'S DAY

1. Serve Mom breakfast in bed, or let the kids help cook a Mother's Day brunch.
2. Look outward and consider if there are women who would be blessed by a visit, flowers, or a phone call.
3. If your adopted child feels the desire to honor his or her birth mother, perhaps you could do so by lighting a candle or planting a flower in her honor.

JUNETEENTH

1. Attend a local Juneteenth celebration in your church or community.
2. Read a biography of black pioneers in American history.

FATHER'S DAY

1. Take an annual camping or hiking trip over Father's Day weekend.
2. Have the kids fill out a fun questionnaire about Dad or Grandpa to give to him. (These are always a hoot in our family!)
3. Go fishing.
4. Ask Dad, "What do *you* want to do today?"

INDEPENDENCE DAY

1. Do some patriotic crafts.
2. Make a patriotic food, such as pancakes with berries and whipped cream or a cake decorated like a flag.
3. Listen to our national anthem.
4. Gather with the neighbors to enjoy sparklers and small fireworks in the street.

HALLOWEEN

1. Host a block party.
2. Provide homemade cider for parents who are walking with their kids by your house.
3. Have a children's costume parade down your street before dark.
4. Honor Martin Luther for Reformation Day by reading his biography, singing "A Mighty Fortress Is Our God," or, on a goofy note, eating gummy worms to teach about the Diet of Worms (the name of Luther's trial).

THANKSGIVING

1. Enjoy reading or listening to stories about the first Thanksgiving.
2. Organize a Thanksgiving craft for the kids.
3. Join a Turkey Trot race or have your own by jogging through the neighborhood.
4. Have the kids decorate the Thanksgiving tables with acorns, pinecones, and colorful leaves from the yard.

LEARNING TRADITIONS

1. Always have a book you're reading aloud together.
2. Install a bird feeder near a window and laminate a bird guide.
3. Make a "Life List" together of the different species of animals you've seen.
4. If you have an annual membership to an aquarium or zoo, give each child a sketchbook to draw animals every time you visit.
5. Offer special prizes if your kids memorize major things (states and capitals, presidents, and so on).
6. Make a family bucket list of educational sites you'd like to visit.
7. Have a special first-day-of-school tradition. We have a "back-to-school fairy" who visits us and puts special educational toys under our pillows.
8. Have a last-day-of-school campout in the backyard.
9. Have family reading time in the afternoon when everyone grabs a book and reads quietly.
10. Have a special first-day-of-summer tradition, such as a pool party and lunch at the pool.

11. Go to the library once a month.
12. When there's an interesting national event, follow it together—an eclipse, hurricane, election, and so on.
13. Work a jigsaw puzzle every Christmas and while on every vacation.
14. Attend an orchestral performance.

SERVICE TRADITIONS

1. When a family you know has a baby, take them a meal.
2. Take valentines or other greeting cards to the neighbors or Daddy.
3. Take flowers or cards to a women's shelter.
4. Totally free act of service: pick a place on the map and pray for the people there.
5. Write on your chalkboard a welcome note to the names of guests coming over to visit.
6. When you have guests over for dinner, have the kids make name cards. People love this!
7. Make muffins or holiday greetings cards for neighbors.
8. After Christmas, hold a Boxing Day auction: everyone in the neighborhood brings something they don't want but is in good condition. Hold an auction, and then take the proceeds to a ministry.
9. Perform a Martin Luther King Jr. day of service.
10. Make cold-weather blessing bags for the homeless to keep in your car.
11. You can also make summer blessing bags; include sunscreen, bottles of water, sunglasses, ChapStick, and other warm-weather must-haves.
12. Volunteer at a soup kitchen or collect soup cans for food banks.

13. Take dinner to someone when that person is sick.
14. Plant a tree for Arbor Day. It's an act of service for future generations.
15. Celebrate the National Day of Prayer.
16. Send flowers for Mother's Day to your mother, mother-in-law, or a mother who may have lost a child.
17. Invite friends to church or open your home for a soup dinner and show a movie about the life of Christ.
18. Clean up a trail or a park. Use rubber gloves and beautify a favorite area.
19. Pi Day Ding Dong Ditch. March 14 is Pi Day. (Pi = 3.14—get it?) How about baking a pie and leaving it as a surprise for a neighbor?
20. Call a veteran you know on Veteran's Day and thank him or her for serving.
21. Send flowers or a special acknowledgment to a military wife or a family who has lost someone who was serving in the military.
22. Serve on a mission trip together.
23. Write letters to grandparents or adopted grandparents.
24. When there is a disaster, add these events to your family prayer time or make a donation to a trusted organization.
25. Bless a teacher in a low-income school by providing classroom supplies or a gift card to purchase things he or she may need for the upcoming year.
26. Buy school supplies for families in need each September.
27. Put on a costume parade through a senior center or assisted-living center at Halloween.
28. Celebrate Saint Nicholas Day by honoring his tradition of giving gifts to needy families.
29. Send teacher appreciation gifts to your children's school and Sunday school teachers.

30. Rake leaves for a neighbor.
31. Fill boxes for Operation Christmas Child.
32. Give a gift to a prisoner's child through the organization Angel Tree.
33. Pray for your friends and family at breakfast or dinner as you receive their Christmas cards.

BIRTHDAYS

1. Fill your child's room with balloons or streamers for a morning surprise.
2. Let the birthday kid have donuts or cake for breakfast.
3. When it's *your* birthday, give a gift to others as an act of kindness.
4. Have the table decorated at breakfast with the gifts, and share words of blessing. ("What I love about you is . . .")[3]
5. Have rite-of-passage birthday traditions. Examples: for the tenth birthday, take a trip with Mom or Dad; for the twelfth birthday, get a nice piece of jewelry, or for the eighteenth, take a very special trip across the country or overseas.
6. Instead of cards, Mom and Dad write notes in a journal for each child; give the journals at their high school graduations.
7. Birthday boy or girl gets to go on a special date with Mom or Dad during that month.
8. Eat lunch with your child at school and, after checking with the teacher about any food allergies classmates might have, take cupcakes to share, following the school's guidelines.
9. Daughters get the number of roses for their age from their daddy.
10. Have a special program your kids do as they transition to adulthood, concluding with a ceremony that recognizes their gifts.

GRANDPARENT TRADITIONS

1. I love the idea of Grandparents Camp, where the grandparents host the grandkids for a week of camp.
2. Grandparents can gift their children a house exchange for the weekend. The grandparents come to the house to watch the grandkids while the parents are at the grandparents' house all weekend.
3. Set up dates with a grandparent. My mom has done this and says it's amazing how the little personalities come to life when they're alone!
4. Grandparents can host Vacation Bible School for the grandkids during the summer.
5. My mother-in-law is the best at sending letters and packages, and I hope I can follow her example one day. For every holiday, she sends an adorable little package with stickers, a gift, and a card for each kid.
6. If you live nearby, grandparents can have the kids spend the night on a dedicated day each week. For example, my cousins spent every Friday night at their grandparents' house.

MARRIAGE TRADITIONS

1. Give a rose each year on the anniversary date you met.
2. Take an anniversary getaway even if it's one night to a local hotel.
3. Weekly date-night-in. Get takeout, spread out on a blanket, and picnic in the living room after the kids go to bed.
4. Put up a chalkboard and leave "thank you" or "I love you because . . ." notes.
5. Revisit spots that are memorable to you.

6. Always greet each other with a kiss.
7. Remember and play your special songs.
8. Do special things when you're apart, like sending a love note in a suitcase or bringing home flowers (or whatever your husband would be grateful to have).
9. Display pictures of when you were dating or engaged, your wedding day, or special trips. These visual traditions are wonderful reminders of your past together.
10. Have a nightly ritual together. My husband and I pray and watch a show together every night.
11. Host a supper club with friends.
12. Write a letter together on New Year's Eve or Christmas Eve of all the things that have happened that year for the two of you. Save the letters.

FAMILY RELATIONSHIP TRADITIONS

1. Have a special plate you use when someone has done something notable—learned a new piece of music, made the honor roll, used the potty, and so forth.
2. Date your kids. Take one child out for one-on-one time every month.
3. Have a "yes day" where you say yes to as many of your kids' requests as you can.
4. Allow one child to stay up extra late and hang out with Mom and Dad. They choose the activity, then pray with them after.
5. If you have appointments together, maximize the time. Go for a special treat after or take along a special game to play.
6. Consider mother-daughter yearly traditions—a tea party, a quilting party, a craft night, a beach outing, and so on. Include the same friends year after year!

7. Consider father-son yearly traditions—a fishing or camping trip, attending a special sports event, and so on.

WORK TRADITIONS

1. Friday cleaning day!
2. Get the house ready for Jesus during Advent.
3. Kids plant a garden each year.
4. Have work parties, with music, games, and a special treat at the end.
5. When kids leave their stuff lying around, they have to grab a chore out of the *work basket*. Just to make things fun, throw a couple of chores in there, like "Hug Mom" or "Write Mom a note that says you love her."
6. Give the kids a *supply allowance* at the beginning of the year. If they lose things—pencils, water bottles, shoes—they have to use their supply allowance. If they have money at the end of the year, they get to keep it!
7. Have dance parties when you do the dishes together.
8. Wash Mom or Dad's car on Mother's Day or Father's Day.

VACATION TRADITIONS

1. Everyone gets a journal to write in or draw the day's events during vacation.
2. Have a craft afternoon where everyone creates a special memento to take home.
3. Have at least one special night with an adult-only dinner.
4. Play games after dinner.
5. Read a book together nightly—your children will always

remember they read that book at the beach (or other vacation spot).

6. Pick a certain candle or essential oil to use for a special trip. You'll always associate that smell with a wonderful time.

7. Consider the power of place and try to visit the same location frequently as a family, whether it's your special rental home or a special lake.

8. Give kids a special car-trip binder or bag with fun things to do during the car ride.

9. Play the license plate game for longer trips. Select and make a list of different states, and if you see a license plate from one of those states, give yourself a fun reward.

10. Listen to a new audiobook in the car.

11. Have a worship service in your vacation rental home if you're away from your church on a Sunday.

12. Take the same family picture every trip (the same person covered to the head in sand, all the kids wearing blue, holding hands looking over a mountain, and so forth).

13. Collect something to take home: shells, rocks, sticks.

14. Have vacation T-shirts made, or make your own with markers or tie-dye.

15. During vacation, give each kid a quarter when you see them being kind or doing something unsolicited and thoughtful. They get to use their quarters for souvenirs.

FAITH TRADITIONS

1. Church!

2. Pray with your kids before bed.

3. Have family devotions after dinner once a week.

4. At Christmas, give each child a new devotional or Christian book.

5. Give each child a special Bible with his or her name on it when each one reaches reading age.
6. Make a list of passages or creeds you'd like your kids to memorize before they leave home, and slowly chip away at this list.
7. Have quiet times with your kids. Give them their "pretend coffee" or tea while you drink yours and you all read your Bibles.
8. Sing a hymn together and say the Lord's Prayer during the bedtime routine.
9. When it snows, have home church. Invite the neighbors, and have coffee!
10. Designate a special Bible verse for each child.
11. Designate a special hymn for each child.

GRIEF TRADITIONS

1. To honor the memory of someone special, consider sponsoring a child with the same birthday as the loved one you lost.
2. Release balloons on the anniversary of a loved one's death or birth.
3. Plant a tree or rosebush in someone's memory.

SPORTS TRADITIONS

1. Celebrate the Super Bowl with an appetizers party.
2. Have a family March Madness basketball competition.
3. Go out for ice cream after baseball games.
4. Attend your local teams' games whenever possible.

5. One family I know always watches football in the garage, no matter the outdoor temperature, so they can throw the football during commercials.
6. Stay up late to watch the college football championship game, World Series, NBA finals, or Super Bowl.

MISCELLANEOUS

1. On nieces' and nephews' birthdays, take them out to dinner and to buy an outfit.
2. Celebrate a special adoption day with a child. Jamie Martin, of the blog *Simple Homeschool*, and her family celebrate Elijah Libya Day and Trishna India Day with their adopted son and daughter, eating the foods and listening to the music of the countries from which they were adopted.
3. If you have adopted a child of another race, find cultural traditions unique for them and celebrate them.
4. Have a *seasonal* tree in your home that you decorate with each changing season or holiday.
5. Have a yearly planning day with Mom and/or Dad when you evaluate individual goals for each family member and for the family as a whole.
6. Celebrate your pet's birthday. (We used to feed our cat a can of tuna with a candle in it.)

TRADITIONS NOT DATE ASSOCIATED

1. Do jigsaw puzzles together.
2. Tell and retell stories from your childhood.
3. Tell stories about your parents or grandparents.

4. Display antiques or special items around your home.

5. Sing or play certain songs that your family loves.

6. Make traditions out of phrases you say often—from the goofy to the serious ("Mommies make mistakes too," for instance).

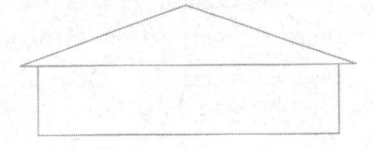

NOTES

Chapter 1: The Worst Day, the Best Gift

1. Sally Clarkson and Sarah Clarkson, *The Lifegiving Home: Creating a Place of Belonging and Becoming* (Carol Stream, IL: Tyndale, 2016), 153.

Chapter 2: Why I Iron the Napkins

1. Edith Schaeffer, *What Is a Family?* (Ada, MI: Baker, 1997), 45.
2. Noël Piper, *Treasuring God in Our Traditions* (Carol Stream, IL: Crossway, 2007), 104.
3. T. David Gordon, lecture, Grove City College, April 2003.
4. Schaeffer, *What Is a Family?*, 195.

Chapter 3: Spontaneity

1. H. Jackson Brown Jr., *P.S. I Love You* (Nashville, TN: Rutledge Hill Press, 1990), 13.
2. Sheila Carlberg, interview with the author, April 8, 2018.
3. Ibid.
4. Edith Schaeffer, *What Is a Family?* (Ada, MI: Baker, 1997), 197.
5. Ideas on this list were brainstormed in conversation with Sheila Carlberg in a personal interview with the author on April 8, 2018.

Chapter 4: Beauty

1. Sally Clarkson and Sarah Clarkson, *The Lifegiving Home: Creating a Place of Belonging and Becoming* (Carol Stream, IL: Tyndale, 2016), 10.
2. Gabrielle Blair, "Family Style," *Magnolia Journal*, no. 6 (Spring 2018), 96.
3. Myquillyn Smith, *The Nesting Place: It Doesn't Have to Be Perfect to Be Beautiful* (Grand Rapids, MI: Zondervan, 2014).
4. Dana K. White, *Decluttering at the Speed of Life: Winning Your Never-Ending Battle with Stuff* (Nashville, TN: W Publishing, 2018), 24.
5. Psalm 127:1 NKJV.
6. Mitchell Owens, "Is it True That Baby Boomers Don't Like Antiques?" *Architectural Digest*, September 8, 2017, https://www.architecturaldigest.com/story/is-it-true-that-baby-boomers-dont-like-antiques.
7. Jessica Smartt, "How to Find Your (Homeschooling) Joy Again," *Smartter Each Day* (blog), September 2017, http://smarttereachday.com/find-homeschooling-joy/.
8. Jessica Smartt, "The Family Hiking Stone," *Wild + Free: Collect* 4, no. 8 (March 2018): 3–4. Available at https://bewildandfree.bigcartel.com/product/collect-content-bundle.
9. This is a paraphrase from William Congreve, *The Mourning Bride*, 1697: "Musick has Charms to sooth a savage Breast, to soften Rocks, or bend a knotted Oak."

Chapter 5: Food

1. Susan Schaeffer Macaulay, *For the Family's Sake: The Value of Home in Everyone's Life* (Wheaton, IL: Crossway, 1999), 127.
2. Joanna Gaines, "Dinner: The Most Important Meal of the Day," *Magnolia Journal* (Spring 2018), 33.
3. Edith Schaeffer, *What Is a Family?* (Ada, MI: Baker, 1997), 96.
4. Sally Clarkson, *The Lifegiving Table* (Carol Stream, IL: Tyndale, 2017), 6.
5. Katie Clark, interview with the author, April 2, 2018.
6. John Haggan, interview with the author, November 11, 2017.

Chapter 6: Holidays

1. Noël Piper, *Treasuring God in Our Traditions* (Carol Stream, IL: Crossway, 2007), 64.
2. Milo Shannon-Thornberry, *The Alternate Celebrations Catalogue* (Cleveland, OH: Pilgrim Press, 1982), 14.
3. Piper, *Treasuring God in Our Traditions*, 94.
4. Amy Frank, personal interview with the author, April 2, 2018.
5. Matthew 25:40.
6. Piper, *Treasuring God in Our Traditions*, 87.
7. Edith Schaeffer, *What Is a Family?* (Ada, MI: Baker, 1997), 193.
8. Page Perry, interview with the author, November 15, 2016.
9. Piper, *Treasuring God in Our Traditions*, 92.
10. Ibid.
11. Jessica Smartt, *Smartter Each Day* (blog), www.smarttereachday .com/memorymakingmomresources.

Chapter 7: Learning

1. Alfred Mercier, quoted in Jamie Whitfield, *Hooked on Literature: How to Make Literature Exciting for Kids* (Waco, TX: Prufrock Press, 2005), 63.
2. Leigh Bortins, *Echo in Celebration: A Call to Home-Centered Education* (Southern Pines, NC: Classical Conversations Multimedia, 2007).
3. Sarah Mackenzie, *The Read-Aloud Family* (Grand Rapids, MI: Zondervan, 2018), 85.
4. Gladys Hunt, *Honey for a Child's Heart*, (Grand Rapids, MI: Zondervan, 2002), 53.
5. Idea from Michelle Bardsley, personal interview with the author, April 21, 2018.
6. Sarah S—, submitted written response to author, "Party Like It's 1999: 25 Traditions You Haven't Thought Of," Becoming Conference, Lake Junaluska, North Carolina, April 21, 2018.

Chapter 8: Service

1. John 15:13 ESV.
2. Edith Schaeffer, *What Is a Family?* (Ada, MI: Baker, 1997), 211.

3. C. S. Lewis, *The Weight of Glory* (New York: HarperOne, 1949), 26.

4. Kristen Welch, *Raising World Changers in a Changing World* (Ada, MI: Baker, 2018), 11.

5. Amy Frank, personal interview with the author, April 2, 2018.

6. Brandon and Emily Todd, personal interview with the author, March 30, 2018.

7. Jeff and Lauren Pyles, personal interview with the author, May 17, 2018.

8. 1 Timothy 5:8.

9. Noël Piper, *Treasuring God in Our Traditions* (Carol Stream, IL: Crossway, 2007), 98.

Chapter 9: Relationships

1. Josh McDowell, "Helping Your Kids to Say No," *Focus on the Family*, October 16, 1987.

2. Bill Jenson, personal interview with the author, October 12, 2017.

3. Author's cousin, personal interview with the author, April 23, 2018.

4. Liesel Johnston, personal interview with the author, November 28, 2017.

5. Becky Mansfield, "How Can You Make Each Child Feel Important?," *Your Modern Family* (blog), December 17, 2017, https://www.yourmodernfamily.com/spending-one-on-one -time-with-your-kids/.

6. For technology management, I recommend Kidslox app for iPhone (https://kidslox.com) and the WasteNoTime program for computers (http://www.bumblebeesystems.com/wastenotime/).

7. Dan Chittock, personal interview with the author, November 20, 2017.

8. Sally Clarkson and Sarah Clarkson, *The Lifegiving Home: Creating a Place of Belonging and Becoming* (Carol Stream, IL: Tyndale, 2016), 73.

9. Jessica Smartt, *Smartter Each Day* (blog), www.smarttereachday .com/memorymakingmomresources.

10. Rachel Jankovic, *Loving the Little Years: Motherhood in the Trenches* (New York: Canon, 2010), 68.

Chapter 10: Work

1. Theodore Roosevelt, speech to the Brotherhood of Locomotive Firemen, Chattanooga, Tennessee, September 8, 1902.
2. Colossians 3:23–24.
3. Stephen Covey, *The 7 Habits of Highly Effective Families* (New York: Golden Books, 1997), 303.
4. Jessica Smartt, "Think You Have Bored Kids? No, Your Kids Aren't Bored—They're Lazy," *Smartter Each Day* (blog), June 2015, http://smarttereachday.com/bored-kids-lazy/.
5. Carole Smartt, e-mail correspondence with the author, May 23, 2018.
6. Daily Lives of Colonists in the 1700s, website based on *My Brother Sam Is Dead*, a novel by James Lincoln Collier and Christopher Collier, https://colonistsdailylives.weebly.com/chores-of-colonial-children.html.
7. You can access this at http://smarttereachday.com/regaining-order-home-rules-consequences-rewards-kids/.

Chapter 11: Rest

1. Edith Schaeffer, *What Is a Family?* (Grand Rapids, MI: Baker, 1975), 95.
2. Ibid., 94.
3. Ibid., 95.
4. Justin Taylor, "Is the Sabbath Still Required for Christians?," *The Gospel Coalition* (blog), October 14, 2010, https://www.thegospelcoalition.org/blogs/justin-taylor/schreiner-qa-is-the-sabbath-still-required-for-christians/.
5. Trevin Wax, "Remember the Sabbath," *The Gospel Coalition* (blog), July 10, 2007, https://www.thegospelcoalition.org/blogs/trevin-wax/remember-the-sabbath/.
6. Gavin Ortlund, "Our Neglected Practice: An Interview with Justin Buzzard on Sabbath Rest," *The Gospel Coalition* (blog), October 22, 2014, https://www.thegospelcoalition.org/article/our-neglected-practice/.
7. Jessica Smartt, *How to Introduce Your Child to Jesus* (Amazon Digital Services, 2014) chapter 4.

8. Laura Ingalls Wilder, *The Long Winter* (New York: HarperCollins, 1940).

9. Russell Cronkhite, *A Return to Sunday Dinner* (Sisters, OR: Multnomah Publishers, 2003), 6.

Chapter 12: Faith

1. Noël Piper, *Treasuring God in Our Traditions* (Carol Stream, IL: Crossway, 2007), 103.

2. You can find recommendations for these resources at www.smartteachday.com/memorymakingmomresources.

3. "The Love of Christ Is Rich and Free," lyrics by William Gadsby, 1852.

4. Cindy Rollins, *A Handbook to Morning Time* (Concord, NC: CiRCE Institute, 2016), 8.

5. Piper, *Treasuring God in Our Traditions*, 44, 48.

6. Ibid., 43.

7. Ibid., 44.

8. Edith Schaeffer, *What Is a Family?* (Ada, MI: Baker, 1997), 137.

9. Ibid., 33.

10. 2 Timothy 4:2.

11. Schaeffer, *What Is a Family?*, 129.

Questions You May Be Asking

1. Brittany Price Brooker, e-mail correspondence with the author, April 8, 2018.

Appendix: 200+ Great Memory-Making Ideas

1. Sheila Carlberg, personal interview with the author, March 1, 2018.

2. Noël Piper, *Treasuring God in Our Traditions* (Carol Stream, IL: Crossway, 2007), 95.

3. Sally Clarkson and Sarah Clarkson, *The Lifegiving Home: Creating a Place of Belonging and Becoming* (Carol Stream, IL: Tyndale, 2016), 73.

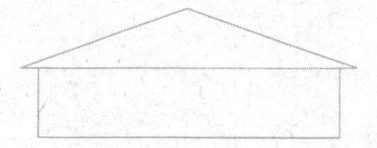

ABOUT THE AUTHOR

JESSICA SMARTT IS A FORMER ENGLISH TEACHER turned homeschooling mama of three. A week after her first baby was born, she began her motherhood blog, *Smartter Each Day*. Jessica and her husband live in beautiful North Carolina, where she loves hikes with the kids (mostly), steaming coffee in the afternoon, family bike rides, and anything that's ever been done to a potato.